Be *There.*

With 7 Skills Critical for Working (and Living) in the Digital Age

Connie Wansbrough

Michaele Robertson

Barry Wansbrough

 FriesenPress

Suite 300 - 990 Fort St
Victoria, BC, V8V 3K2
Canada

www.friesenpress.com

Available for sale at www.skillpod.ca.

Contact the Skillpod office directly regarding special quantity discounts for bulk purchases for training or educational needs. Elements of the book can be customized to your needs. For details, contact info@skillpod.ca.

Published by Skillpod, Inc.
Toronto, Canada.

More information about Skillpod and the authors can be found at skillpod.ca.

ISBN
978-1-5255-5417-9 (Hardcover)
978-1-5255-5418-6 (Paperback)
978-1-5255-5419-3 (eBook)

1. Business & Economics, Careers

Distributed to the trade by The Ingram Book Company

Table of Contents

Preface 6

Introduction: What are Executive Skills
   (And Why They Matter). 8

Skillpod 7 Skills 9

Getting *There*: Program & Benefits. 10

Skillpod Learning Program. 11

Personal Learning Preferences. 12

My Skillpod Profile 14

How Well Do You Know Your Skills 15

Skill 1: Smarter Learning. 16

Skill 2: Selfwork 30

Skill 3: Communication. 44

Skill 4: Teamwork 58

Skill 5: Information Management. 72

Skill 6: Strategic Thinking 86

Skill 7: Design & Innovation 100

How Well Do You Know Your Skills Now?. 115

Appendix 1: The PLP 116

Appendix 2: Creating a Portfolio Entry 120

Preface

Over many years of working with K-12 learners, Michaele and Barry learned some valuable lessons from their students about how students learn best. These lessons helped them to support school programming that put an inquiring learner and a balance of skills and content at the centre of the schools they helped to shape.

Upon retirement, they had time to consider the world beyond school walls and the education young people needed to succeed in that world. Their reading and the interviews they conducted revealed that there was profound agreement on one key issue: education is the driver of wealth creation and prosperity. The countries that best prepare their young people for work in a global context will have the advantage.

There is consensus among international and national educators at all levels, as well as economists, commentators, and thought leaders in many fields, about what knowledge, skills, and dispositions will count as progress toward this goal. However packaged, these attributes generally include:

- ► local and global civic responsibility
- ► creating and maintaining relationships
- ► working together locally or over distance
- ► learning in different contexts
- ► thinking in a complex way
- ► inventing or creating

Teachers agree that these skills are critical, but are stymied by the how of it all – how to find time, how to assess the skills, and how to make them significant to students and parents. This is the problem Michaele and Barry set out to address by creating LIKA, the precursor to Skillpod.

In 2018, Connie, a design strategist and college professor, joined the team. LIKA relaunched as Skillpod, Inc., reorienting the content to focus on the eighteen-to-twenty-five-year-old cohort. The three of them saw an urgency with this group of young people as they headed out into their first career jobs anxious about what lay ahead. Those who were interviewed knew that these skills were important, but they were also stymied when it came to systematically building them, especially when so many were starting their careers working freelance or contract-to-contract, with little mentoring or on-the-job guidance.

This workbook is not meant to be a traditional textbook. Connie, Michaele, and Barry saw a need for a simple, engaging book that is more practical than theoretical. With its structured approach, people can move forward and see progress quickly. The model and methodology allow people to work through the material on their own, in a classroom, or with a coach. The intention is that the workbook be mature, challenging, and engaging.

The overarching goal of Skillpod is to help (young) people meet the challenge of becoming the flexible, resilient, self-directed, and curious people they need to be in order to ensure their best future while building prosperity for themselves and their communities.

We would like to thank many people who have enthusiastically and generously helped us along our way, including:

- The supportive leadership and staff at George Brown College, Toronto, who provided feedback and encouragement.

- The first set of students who attended our workshops and validated the approach.

- The students since then who have tested and provided feedback on materials, particularly David Ho Sang, for beta testing the materials and for his unflagging enthusiasm.

- Karen Ford for her eagle eye and help with copy editing.

- Shanna Nozdryn for her design help from the earliest LIKA days.

- Eunice Joaquin for her Skillpod branding vision and Samantha Bullis for additional branding work and the concept and layout of this workbook.

- Chris Wansbrough, whose generous support has allowed the development of this material.

- Joan VanDuzer, whose generous support allowed for the design and production of this workbook.

- Eric Lowy, who has printed many rough copies, read many rough drafts, and been a loyal sounding board.

- Ben, for reminding us to have a sense of humour and that adults should practise what they preach. And to his cousins, Diego, Daniela, Kate and Victor, whose working futures depend on acquiring the skills in this book.

- Kaitlin and Melissa, who have provided constant inspiration with all they do and accomplish.

INTRODUCTION
What are Executive Skills (And Why They Matter)?

(Young) people today are facing economic uncertainty. Old business models are out and new, disruptive models are growing. These new models require flexible, adaptable, agile, and transferable social and cognitive (thinking) executive skills. In order to be competitive and thrive in our emerging economy, we need to be better thinkers, learners, and communicators. Literacy and numeracy are important but executive skills including information technology and management skills are growing in value.

Most of the schooling years are taken up with core knowledge learning. Often, those agendas are so full that they build more anxiety than competency. Carving out the space for developing important workplace-related skills is left almost entirely to the individual, yet experts identify these skills as representing 50% of what these youth need for future success.

Skillpod helps prepare for employment, self-employment, or career advancement by helping people hone and share their own unique skills for the entrepreneurial and digital economy.

Demand for these skills is overwhelming and precise.

Learning priorities that executives and hiring managers value most highly cut across majors.

The more prepared the minds are that address current and future issues, the better off everyone will be. In the past, societies were led by very small groups of the best-educated citizens. Social and economic change was sparked by challenges to existing political systems. Today, change is multi-faceted and faster than ever. The main drivers of change are the immense data banks, new ideas, and technologies. The impact of economic change is competing with climate change – improving one adversely impacts the other in a zero-sum game. Additionally, the liberal democracies that built record prosperity are now challenged by a wave of nationalist populism that requires new thought to understand. Collaboration and communication – the keys to democracy – are under threat. The ability to work and problem-solve together calls for a combination of the skills in this workbook. In our social, economic and political conditions, it is the combination of hard knowledge and soft executive skills (social and cognitive) that is the formula for success.

Skillpod addresses each one of the skills listed in the graph below in an efficient, engaging, and systematic way.

Very Important* Skills for Recent College Graduates We Are Hiring

Business executives **Hiring Managers**

Skill	Business executives	Hiring Managers
Able to effectively communicate orally	80%	90%
Critical thinking/analytical reasoning	78%	84%
Ethical judgement and decision-making	77%	87%
Able to work effectively in teams	77%	87%
Able to work independently (prioritize, manage time)	77%	85%
Self-motivated, initiative, proactive: ideas/solutions	76%	85%
Able to communicate effectively in writing	76%	78%
Can apply knowledge/skills to real-world settings	76%	87%

*8-10 ratings on a 0-to-10 scale. 15 outcomes tested

Skillpod Skills

Skill 1: Smarter Learning

It is possible to improve one's learning capacity. Artificial Intelligence (AI) and quantum computers will replace at least 50% of existing jobs because of the new knowledge created in the coming years. Future success will depend on how well and effectively people can learn over their entire working lives. It is a necessary challenge for people to think about learning not as a fixed asset but as a skill.

Skill 2: Selfwork

Full-time jobs are becoming harder to find in the gig economy requiring a renewed emphasis on Selfwork skills. There is less on-the-job mentoring, which means there is a greater need for self-reliance and self-motivation. The dominance of social media and celebrity culture makes finding your own vision a particular challenge and more important now than ever.

Skill 3: Communication

Social media has democratized communication. With a smartphone in hand, anyone can communicate with anyone or everyone. Good communicators will consider the context and audience, be careful to distinguish personal from professional information, and control how and where information is distributed.

Skill 4: Teamwork

With very few exceptions, good teams outperform individual efforts. Group or team success depends on all members understanding and respecting roles. Teams are expected to work fluidly in person and also remotely, which requires sophisticated information management and communication skills.

Skill 5: Information Management

Google can find millions of responses in fractions of seconds. With AI and quantum computers, the speed and volume of data will only increase. The question now is not how much information is available, but what sources of information to track and what information to protect. The top item to protect is personal data. Understanding which online sources give the best quality information with the least risk is paramount.

Skill 6: Strategic Thinking

People's abilities to communicate in a strategic way, to understand what counts as good evidence for an argument, and to reach defensible conclusions are highly valued. Strategic thinking skills combined with strong teamwork and communication skills are required to move into leadership positions.

Skill 7: Design & Innovation

Design methodology is front and centre of the new economy, impacting everything from products to systems. It is a process for developing new things, and better goods and services. With manufacturing shifting from North America and Europe to other countries, what is left to create is wealth or what is called "Think" innovation. This is a huge shift in thinking in an area that has, in the past, been the exclusive domain of the creative class.

Getting *There*

It is important to keep in mind that these skills are not an end in themselves. Honing executive skills enables people to use hard skills (core subject learning) effectively in the Digital Age. The key is to be able to demonstrate mastery of both types of skills.

Skills take practice, so it is our hope that once you understand what actions will make you more skillful, you will practise them until they become second nature and that you will document your progress in a digital curriculum vitae (CV), portfolio, or website. As job definitions become more specific, we believe that search algorithms will favour skills such as these and that interviews will favour candidates who command the language to discuss their skills at a deep level.

Think of these skills as the "keywords" or differentiators for any search in which the field is populated by candidates with the same knowledge as you, but whose skills are less developed. You will stand out as a candidate, whether your CV is processed by hand or algorithm. When you are interviewed, your ability to discuss these skills and their component parts will help you speak with confidence about the value you can bring to an organization and help you land the job you want.

As a result of doing the work, you will have a portfolio of marketable and transferable skills that are supported with concrete examples of performance.

Benefits of Skillpod:

Working through the Skillpod program will help you:

- build knowledge about our 7 skills and understand why they are important
- assess and deepen your competency in each skill
- build evidence of your skills, drawing from your own life experiences and the world around you
- develop language to be able to talk about your experiences and interests from a skills perspective
- set personal and professional goals
- present yourself with confidence to potential employers or entrepreneurial funders

Beware! Completing the Skillpod program may result in:

- increased confidence
- improved ability to think and learn more effectively
- improved ability to manage yourself more productively
- preparation for career opportunities
- career advancement

Skillpod Learning Program

There are other skills and competencies that could have been included. We have carefully chosen ones we consider to be fundamental to most situations. The Skillpod skills, definitions, competencies, and exercises are meant to provide you with a methodology and starting point for your skills-based learning.

Our Learning Method

Scenario-Based Learning

For each skill, we provide background information, including the Skillpod definition of the skill. Each skill is further defined by four main "competencies," or key elements. We then provide a scenario-based learning program that focuses on building the knowledge of each competency. You will be asked to reflect and write about each competency after completing the scenario. Once you've completed the four scenario-based exercises for a particular skill, you will be ready to create a digital portfolio entry. You will be asked to define the skill in your own words, articulate why it's valued, and provide an example based on your knowledge and experience using the language of the competencies.

Self-Assessment

After finishing a skill chapter, you will complete a self-assessment to clearly see areas of strength and areas in need of further development. In this self-assessment, you will read and respond to eight questions relating to each skill. The responses are either YES or NOT YET. If you respond YES, move on to the next skill. If you respond NOT YET, make a note of it. If this is a priority skill for you, investigate the exercises in the Toolbox section that follows each chapter for ways to deepen your mastery of this skill.

Demonstrating Your Expertise – Digital Portfolio

The final step is to create a digital portfolio entry. For this you will use an example you have selected, find or create an image that captures this example, and post this portfolio piece on a digital platform of your choice (e.g., personal website, LinkedIn, Google doc). If you want to go an extra mile, you can ask someone to endorse your skill-based portfolio entry, similar to a "recommendation" on LinkedIn. This endorsement is most useful if you choose someone senior to you (e.g., a teacher, boss, supervisor, coach). There is a guide to creating a portfolio entry in the appendix of this workbook.

What are Personal Learning Preferences?

The Personal Learning Preferences (PLP) self-assessment is the first competency in the Smarter Learning skill. The foundation of learning is understanding yourself. This assessment can be used as a tool to help you leverage your strengths when you need to learn something new or to help you complete a project or task. Knowing your PLP can help reduce frustration and increase success. This inventory of strengths is neither static nor permanent. It will evolve as you grow, learn, and respond to dynamics in your environment.

As the first step, complete the assessment at www.skillpod.ca or see Appendix I for more information about the PLP.

Key sources of information that factor into the PLP are your role preferences, multiple intelligences and personal interests.

Elements of the PLP

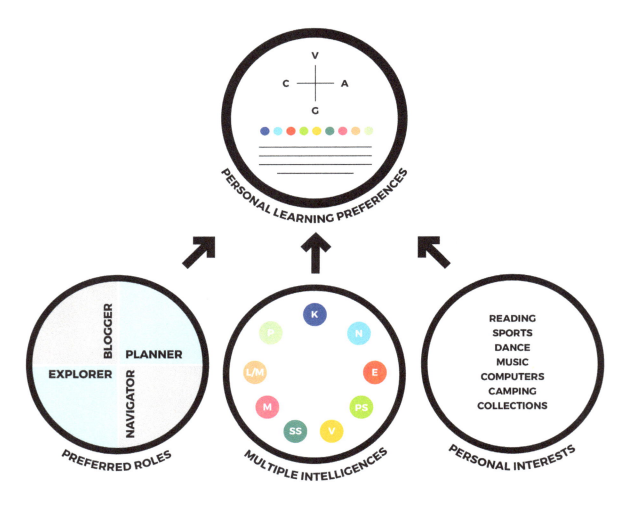

Skillpod's Personal Learning Preferences Quadrants

Your learning preferences will be described as falling into four areas, which we call quadrants. Each quadrant relates to a specific set of strengths. The combined quadrants include all skills that are required to complete a project or task.

Verbal/Linguistic
Words/Reading/Speaking

Quadrant 2
Verbal – Concrete

Learns best through words and "hands-on" activities. Thinks about relationships.

Examples: salespersons, coaches, promoters, content creators, politicians, actors, novelists, educators, social services workers.

Quadrant 1
Verbal – Abstract

Learns best through words and imagination. Thinks logically.

Examples: mathematicians, financial analysts, legal services, accountants, medical researchers, software developers and information managers. Poets and physicists are here and often excel in Q4 traits as well.

Concrete
Real Life/
Doing

Abstract
Imagination/
Thinking

Quadrant 3
Graphic - Concrete

Learns best through diagrams, doing and making.

Examples: engineers, craftspeople, athletes, chefs, dancers, musicians, explorers, security professionals, all trades, personal services workers.

Quadrant 4
Graphic - Abstract

Learns best through diagrams and using imagination.

Examples: artists, designers, architects, health care professionals, entrepreneurs and business consultants. Physicists and poets may be here and often excel in Q1 traits as well.

Graphic/Visual
Pictures/Images/Diagrams

My Skillpod Profile

Use this page to track your skill development. Each ray represents one skill. Each box in the ray represents one competency. Fill them in as you complete each section.

How Well Do You Know Your Skills?

The questions below are the four most common interview questions. They all ask for you to articulate your skills. Please write responses in full sentences.

Imagine you are applying for a job as a junior employee at your dream firm. How would you answer these question right now?

Name:

1 **Tell me about yourself.**
What are the first three things that you would say if someone asked you about you?

1.

2.

3.

2 **What are your top three strengths?**

1.

2.

3.

3 **What weaknesses do you have?**

1.

2.

4 **What is the number-one value you could bring to this organization?**
Why should I consider hiring you?

1.

SMARTER LEARNING

Definition: Learning is the change in one's behaviour or knowledge which comes about as a result of experience.

Introduction

Until recently there was a belief and confidence that school learning was what you needed to prepare for a (non-trade related) career. The academic model was based on listening, reading, memorizing and passing tests. It wasn't necessary to spend time understanding how we learn. That era is over. We do not know what the employment future will be but knowing how you learn best will be a big help with any new challenge.

We now know that we all learn in different ways, and sometimes individuals have different methods of learning depending on the job they need to do.

The Skillpod Smarter Learning module is based on understanding yourself as a learner so that you can start to learn faster and design learning in a way that best suits your personal needs. It will help you learn from past successes and understand what works best for you.

Competencies:

1 **Knowing yourself as a learner**
Complete the PLP for an understanding of your learning preferences. The better you know yourself, the smarter and faster you can learn. (See Appendix 1)

2 **Cultivating a growth mindset**
A growth mindset is more than being openminded. It is a belief that you are capable of improving if you apply effort.

3 **Achieving your goals**
Creating well-defined goals will help structure your learning.

4 **Harnessing the power of failure**
Fear of failure prevents learning. Failure must be reframed as an opportunity for learning.

What employers value about strong Smarter Learning skills:

► Willingness to learn

► Resilience

► Resourcefulness

► Adaptability

► Ability to learn from others

What entrepreneurs value about strong Smarter Learning skills:

► Ability to tackle new challenges

► Efficient tactics

► Learning from failure

► Perseverance

► Initiative

Knowing yourself as a learner

Jim was hired to help a local politician get re-elected. He had a college certificate in general business practice, and a Personal Learning Preference (PLP) that leaned to the Q3, concrete/graphic preference quadrant. When Jim arrived at the office, he received a large file of background documents and instructions which detailed his responsibilities. The politician was mostly on the road, building community support. Jim was left with one office colleague and some volunteers at headquarters. Jim was not a person comfortable with text as much as he was with graphic material and the thought of wading through the file was daunting - he wanted to get things done.

Jim did not read the file, nor did he find someone more comfortable with textual material to help him.

Jim contacted the election administrative official, the returning officer, to make sure the dates and rules of the campaign were followed. He gave an assistant the job of organizing the volunteers for the canvassing, and he took on the job of fundraising with the candidate. Jim was a personable guy and people were happy to see him. What was not so positive was that Jim lacked any knowledge of the riding, the procedures that had historically been in place or, most vitally, the policies of his boss. All that material had been in the file which Jim had decided not to read. The result was that Jim could not campaign effectively with his boss, could not answer questions, help with briefings or speak to the press or local associations on behalf of the riding office. The candidate lost the election.

Your initial analysis (select all that apply)

☐ Jim did not understand himself as a learner

☐ Jim understood what he needed to learn

☐ Jim's assistant was unhelpful

☐ Jim had the wrong learning profile for the job

☐ The politician was unhelpful

Skillpod Insight

Two key elements of this scenario are knowing how to learn smarter using one's strengths and initiating new learning when needed. Jim missed both elements. Essentially, because it is not his strength, he turns his back on a critical task and, by doing so, limits his effectiveness. Had he understood the idea of learning preferences and how to make the most of individual differences, he could have been better prepared to compensate for his gaps in skill. Jim had the ability to succeed, but not the plan or understanding of how to leverage strengths to get the job done.

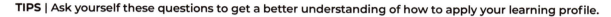

TIPS | Ask yourself these questions to get a better understanding of how to apply your learning profile.

- ▶ Have I completed and understood my PLP? If not, go to www.skillpod.ca and complete the PLP
- ▶ Can I recognize when there is an important new learning opportunity?
- ▶ Do I have strategies for engaging people with different learning profiles?
- ▶ Can I recognize, understand and appreciate how other's different learning profiles can help me?
- ▶ Have I constructed a model or system for how I can be a smarter learner?

Reflection:

Take a minute to reflect on a situation where you effectively used your learning strengths or wish that you had. Write a few lines here.

DONE go back to your profile page and fill in a Smarter Learning block or
NOT YET continue to the next scenario or jump to the Toolbox at the end of the chapter for more practice.

Cultivating a growth mindset

Jasper and Archie were friends who grew up in the rural community of Inglenook, a lovely waterside town with a strong heritage of cottaging and resorts. Jasper and Archie had both worked for their fathers and other builders in the area as they grew up and they knew the community well, They saw it changing from a traditional "family at the cottage for the summer" venue to a place attractive to shorter-term rentals. They watched as old family cottages were rented by the month and listened to people complain about the issues of maintenance, supervision and vetting renters. They saw an opportunity for a property management business and had soon persuaded their families and the bank to help them get started.

At first things went well and Jasper, particularly, was happy to see things progressing in a manageable way. Archie, however, could see that the real opportunity was an integrated services model, in which additional offerings such as cleaning, laundry, grounds and boat maintenance and security would all be extremely attractive. In order to realize Archie's vision, it became apparent that the two of them would have to hire more people and, in order to meet that payroll, would have to commit to a loan from their families and work hard to find clients.

When Jasper looked ahead, he saw the risk of financial uncertainty. He did not think they had the skills and knowledge or clients to make this expansion viable. When Archie looked ahead, he saw the changing population who had more income and needed on-the-ground help both to rent and to secure their investments. Most of all, he knew that the cottage owners who would be their clients, knew their families and trusted them both.

Archie could not get Jasper to share his mindset. Jasper believed that rentals were the limit of what they should take on as the expanded business model required a very different set of skills. They parted and remained friends. Archie's parents were eventually won over by his careful planning, strong local relationships and the positive results he achieved. With hard work and commitment, Archie continued to develop, grow and strengthen the business.

Your initial analysis (select all that apply)

☐ Archie took a big risk and was lucky

☐ On balance, Jasper made the more sensible choice

☐ Jasper saw things in the future turning out as they were in the present

☐ Personal service is a growing cultural need

☐ Archie's parents could have been more helpful

Skillpod Insight

Most people have fixed mindsets and have to work to deliberately move to a growth mindset. A growth mindset is not just about being positive. It is a process and mindset that allows for growth (learning) to happen. Jasper could not picture the same positive future for their efforts that Archie could. He was more focused on what might go wrong – the limitations they faced, which were certainly there. His mindset was fixed. He believed that things are best to continue as they have been. Archie, on the other hand, could see a different future based on trends already evident, and was eager to collaborate with others to grow the business. He worked to cultivate a growth mindset, believing in his vision and his ability to make the vision real.

TIPS | Ask yourself these questions to get better at cultivating a growth mindset.

- ▸ Am I aware of the signs that I am thinking with a fixed mindset?
- ▸ When I am in a fixed mindset, what elements do I need to work to overcome?
- ▸ Can I envision myself succeeding in a task?
- ▸ Am I able to identify risk and potential for failure and take steps to mitigate it?
- ▸ Do I know how to ask for help when I have hit a roadblock?
- ▸ Am I open to feedback?
- ▸ Do I know how to leverage my network to help me succeed in a task/situation?

Reflection:

Take a minute to reflect on a situation where you effectively used your growth mindset or wish that you had. Write a few lines here.

DONE go back to your profile page and fill in a Smarter Learning block or
NOT YET continue to the next scenario or jump to the Toolbox at the end of the chapter for more practice.

SCENARIO 3
Achieving your goals

Jean was tasked by her bosses to meet a goal that would reduce, and hopefully eliminate, bullying and harassment in her workplace. This had been a very difficult issue in her company because women and the LGBTQ employees were vulnerable both to harassment and to a glass ceiling for promotions. When the evidence was presented to the bosses they were reluctantly forced to act. They appointed Jean to lead the project, believing that she had the confidence of her colleagues. Jean had no direct experience and was facing a steep learning curve ahead.

Jean had a very sensitive task. To further complicate matters, the boss of a close competitor had recently been fired for inappropriate behaviour with female employees. The whole climate Jean was working within was negative.

Jean faced the dilemma of whether to direct her energy to investigating the historical negative climate her bosses had allowed to go unchecked, or to work on a company policy that would lay out very clearly the professional behaviour necessary to remain an employee of the company. Where should her time and energy go? Jean was aware that she lacked the background either to conduct an investigation or to forge a new company policy. Many of her colleagues across the company were anxious to go after the perpetrators – to nail them!

After a lot of thought and some good advice, Jean decided that it was more important to have the policy. With a policy in place, offenders at any level of the company could be held accountable. Jean knew she had to make a careful plan, learning all she could from trusted sources, to ensure the policy would protect everyone in the workplace.

Your initial analysis (select all that apply)

- ☐ Jean should have investigated the perpetrators
- ☐ Jean should have declined the challenge
- ☐ Her colleagues should have had more say in the process
- ☐ Jean is wise to think long-term about a serious problem
- ☐ Jean was the wrong person to lead this task

Skillpod Insight

Having a clear goal, familiarity with her PLP, and understanding the PLP model of including all relevant Quadrant skills (Q1 - research, Q2 - communicating, Q3 - prototyping and Q4 - visualizing/big picture thinking) will help Jean shape a plan for what needs to be learned.

In order to learn fastest and best about the given task, Jean needs to focus her efforts on the research mind (Q1), as she starts creating the new policy. Next, she will need to focus on communicating this new policy which requires different skills (Q2). Having a clear goal will help Jean inventory what relevant skills, strengths and knowledge she already has and assess gaps would need to be filled by new learning or leaning on others. In this way, she can identify new learning needs efficiently and quickly fill the gaps. Well-defined goals will help structure any new learning.

TIPS | Ask yourself these questions to get better at achieving your goals.

- ▸ Have I planned and set goals? Is my goal clear?
- ▸ Can I anticipate what needs to be learned in order to reach my goal?
- ▸ Have I considered my PLP and the PLP model in my plan?
- ▸ Have I anticipated and planned for obstacles along the way?
- ▸ How would I deal with radically different views of others involved in achieving the goal?
- ▸ What role does communication play in the exercise?

Reflection:

Take a minute to reflect on a situation where having a clearer goal would have added to your success. Write a few lines here.

DONE go back to your profile page and fill in a Smarter Learning block or
NOT YET continue to the next scenario or jump to the Toolbox at the end of the chapter for more practice.

SCENARIO 4
Harnessing the power of failure

After World War II, Japan started to make goods for export that were considered by many to be 'cheap foreign imports'. The quality of their goods was very low. Take Japanese cars as an example. In Japan, the quality of the manufacturing, design and materials were all at a minimal level after the war. By contrast, in North America, materials and design were of a higher quality and the manufacturing process was more sophisticated. When cars came off the production lines they faced a final inspection. If faults were found, the car was sent back.

By the 70s and 80s, the quality of North American cars had declined. Automaker Ford suffered from the tagline, 'rusty Fords'. The winter road salting was taking its toll and the materials could not stand up to it. At the same time, the Japanese car industry, acting as a national team, hired statistical expert W.

Edwards Deming to help them improve. His method was to eliminate error by building teams of workers to correct errors along the production line. As a result, the cars came off the line without faults that needed to be sent back. This was a much more efficient manufacturing process than the final inspection model, used in North America. In order to improve quality, the Japanese embraced failure by recognizing the separate errors along the assembly line and eliminating them where they occured. As a result, their cars became the highest quality cars of the era.

The Japanese success formula became the global model for excellence in car production, setting new global standards. The methodical identification of error and its correction, on the spot and without blame, is a great example of harnessing the power of failure.

Your initial analysis (select all that apply)

- ☐ Failure is better than not trying
- ☐ Only error can help you improve
- ☐ Everyone experiences failure – it is a positive in life
- ☐ To be successful, you have to avoid failure
- ☐ Too many people are obsessed with getting it right

Skillpod Insight

Failure and error are facts of life. What matters is how we frame them. What is interesting about the Edwards Deming story is that he was able to change the way the Japanese thought about error – to make it something people wanted to find so that they could correct it. He made error manageable, by eliminating it step-by-step.

We spend a lot of time in school and business confronting failure, and usually it means loss of standing. Almost all of us think that errors are bad. If error and failure are negative, we won't try new things. Much has been learned from a good try and a clear miss.

TIPS | Ask yourself these questions to get better at learning from failure.

- ▶   Do I fear failure? If so, why?
- ▶   Do I anticipate the consequences of failure?
- ▶   Do I anticipate the consequences of avoiding failure?
- ▶   Do I have strategies for managing errors in my work and life?
- ▶   What strategy do I have for not being discouraged by a failure?

Reflection:

Take a minute to reflect on a situation where you have used failure as a learning experience. Write a few lines here.

DONE go back to your profile page and fill in a Smarter Learning block or
NOT YET continue to the next scenario or jump to the Toolbox at the end of the chapter for more practice.

Congratulations!

You have completed the Smarter Learning skill.

Self-Assessment:

Complete the following questions to assess your understanding of the material.

	COMPETENCY	YES	NOT YET
1	I can create learning situations that make the most of my learning strengths.		
1	I am good at initiating the learning of new things when I need to.		
2	I willingly seek help from other people or consult sources of information when I am stuck.		
2	I can picture myself succeeding in a role or in a task.		
3	I can plan and set learning goals.		
3	I am good at anticipating what I need to learn next.		
4	Having clear goals helps me persist through obstacles.		
4	I have been able to use failure as a learning experience.		

If you have answered **YES** to these questions, move on to the Smarter Learning portfolio entry page. If you have answered **NOT YET,** reflect on where you are running into roadblocks in your understanding of the related competency and what you can do to address this. Take a look a the Toolbox on the next page and try some of the exercises to deepen your understanding or mastery of the skill.

The Toolbox

Use the following activities to dig deeper and continue to build your Smarter Learning skills.

Knowing yourself as a learner: (est. 30 min.)

Find one thing you would like to know better – e.g. a language, software, sport or skill or something else you are interested in. From your PLP identify the quadrants that would best support the learning for that item. From your results graph, see how your strengths match the new learning task. Check the internet for ideas on learning things you find difficult – how your strengths can be used in different ways to learn.

Cultivating a growth mindset: (est. 15 min.)

The first step of cultivating a growth mindset is to establish a goal and to allow yourself to visualize success. Take one important goal you have yet to achieve – e.g. a physical goal, receiving an important promotion, or finding a supporter for something you are developing. Let's say you have an interview for a new job. Do you know what the interviewer wants to see and hear? How much do you know about the company and the position to be filled? What evidence, from your portfolio, do you have to present if needed? In other words, how well prepared are you to realistically visualize your success? One thing that we sometimes forget, and it is true for taking tests or winning a game, is to clear the mind of as much noise as possible. Clear concentration is the key. It is the first principle of mental clarity, and that is a big plus for success.

Achieving your goals: (est. 1 hour +)

The key to achieving your goals is making sure you have a solid path to success. Pick one goal for a specific outcome you want, e.g. a new job, a sports victory, or a committee to join. First, think about what you already know that can help you get to this goal. Outline what else you will need to learn in order to get there. Identify areas which need help. Ask a colleague or friend for feedback on your plan. What are you missing and who can help you? What will your learning plan look like now? Try this with various goals.

Harnessing the power of failure: (est. 30 min.)

We have all failed at many things, so finding examples should not be a problem. The question is what have we learned from them? Take one significant failure you have had. There may be nothing you can do about it now, but is there something you can learn from it for the future? We often tend to lay blame for a failure, and that is natural but unhelpful. What is important is what we learn from it. With this in mind, pick one major failure you have had and write down what you have learned from the experience. If you could build several lessons from this, even better. Over time, with practice, you will develop a new habit of seeing and valuing these setbacks not as failures but as positive learning experiences.

Smarter Learning Portfolio Entry

You are ready to create a portfolio piece that captures your own unique Smarter Learning skill. Include skills-based language from the table below in your writing.

COMPETENCIES	ASSETS ("I...")
Knowing yourself as a learner	· can modify learning tactics · can initiate learning when needed
Cultivating a growth mindset	· am open to feedback · can visualize success
Achieving your goals	· can plan goals · anticipate learning needs
Harnessing the power of failure	· see failure as learning · persist

STEP 1:

DEFINE
In your own words, define Smarter Learning.

"For example, I see Smarter Learning as a combination of ..."

STEP 1 (Continued):

DEMONSTRATE:
Using skills-based language, describe one specific experience that captures your skill in this area.

If you are stuck for what to write in your portfolio, think about including some of these phrases like, "I can visualize success".

ARTICULATE:
Why would an employer value your unique Smarter Learning skills?

STEP 2:

CREATE
Use the portfolio guidelines in the appendix to create a Smarter Learning portfolio entry.

STEP 3:

SHARE!
Feature this skill on your social media feed, your website, LinkedIn or online portfolio.

SKILL 2:
SELFWORK

Selfwork is the skill of knowing ourselves well enough to achieve our goals by building patterns of behaviour that move us closer to who we want to become.

Introduction

Stephen Covey, author of *The 7 Habits of Highly Effective People*, would say that there is only one thing that we can control and that is ourselves. Although it might seem obvious, we don't always put as much emphasis or effort on managing or developing ourselves as we do on managing others or developing relationships with others.

We are including four competencies that can help develop strong intrapersonal skills.

Competencies:

1 Valuing self and others
Respect is the granting of value to the experiences, beliefs, needs and possessions of others that is at least equal to the value given one's own experiences, beliefs, needs and possessions.

2 Demonstrating reliability
This is a key element of trust. You want to be known as a person who keeps commitments. You build this reputation through effort and practice as you would any skill.

3 Visualizing a positive future
You can imagine a future for yourself of positive and realistic accomplishment and of relationships that are supportive and happy.

4 Showing resilience
Cultivate the ability to motivate yourself – it isn't someone else's responsibility.

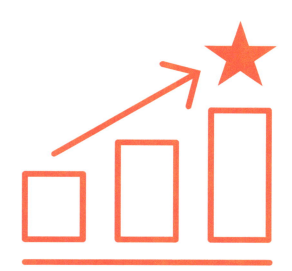

What employers value about strong Selfwork skills:

- ► Reliability
- ► Integrity
- ► Organization
- ► Emotional intelligence
- ► Self-knowledge/ Self-worth
- ► Persistence/ Future-orientation

What entrepreneurs value about strong Selfwork skills:

- ► Resilience
- ► Self knowledge/self worth
- ► Perseverance
- ► Initiative
- ► Vision/future orientation
- ► Self-control

SCENARIO 1
Valuing self and others

Nasir is the president of a current affairs club in a large city. One of his responsibilities is to help plan and give final approval on a list of monthly speakers who address complex issues of the moment. The monthly talks are hosted by the club for the public at no cost and frequently draw large crowds.

Nasir and his committee work hard to ensure the speakers are knowledgeable and address truly current issues. Their ability to attract both speakers and enthusiastic audience members is helped by the presence of a university in their city which has an active political science department.

While considering the proposed list, Nasir notices that one of the speakers is well known for criticizing the government's liberal immigration policies which she sees as threatening existing norms and beliefs. A member of the club proposes to invite this speaker after learning that she will be speaking at the local university, an invitation which has provoked controversy in the university community. Nasir knows her earlier appearances in other cities have led to confrontations. He voices his hesitation and finds club members sharply divided – some advocating for the invitation on the grounds of free speech, and others against the invitation on the grounds that her comments could provoke targeted attacks on visible minorities. Unable to to find a majority view, he realizes the decision is his to make. There are people on both sides of the issue whom he respects. The situation is further complicated by the fact that he himself is an immigrant.

What should he do?

Your initial analysis (select all that apply)

☐ Cancel the invitation

☐ Treat this as if it were not controversial and go ahead with the usual arrangements

☐ Hold the event for club members only

☐ Advertise the university event as a replacement for the club event

☐ Set up a panel discussion which represents a range of views

Skillpod Insight

Nasir's dilemma illustrates how complicated it can be to balance competing points of view respectfully. One could argue that he is respecting some points of view, whichever option he choses. Nasir decides to give priority to respecting the club's mandate to provide public education on issues. He decides to run a panel discussion with a variety of expert views. The speaker in question will be invited to participate on that panel. The event will be, as usual, open to the public. Nasir will take added steps to ensure the meeting is orderly and safe for all who attend. He will also visualize obstacles, potential sources of conflict and think through his options for reactions to ensure that he is prepared to exercise self-control in his moderating of the event.

TIPS | **Before taking action that may have an impact on others, here are some things to consider to ensure you are being as respectful of others as possible:**

- ▶ Have I faced my own biases before taking any action?

- ▶ Have I taken the time to understand different points of view in a respectful manner?

- ▶ Have I consulted with others who could help me think through various options?

- ▶ Have I determined whether all points of view will be of equal weight in making a decision?

- ▶ Have I considered whether there is an institutional vision or mission or an organizational mandate that might help me decide on a respectful course of action?

Reflection:

Take a minute to reflect on a situation in which either respect for self or respect for others was absent.
Write a few lines here.

DONE go back to your profile page and fill in a Selfwork block or
NOT YET continue to the next scenario or jump to the Toolbox at the end of the chapter for more practice.

SCENARIO 2
Demonstrating reliability

In many respects, Jared could be a sales star. Articulate and polished, with a quick wit and good sense of humour, he makes customers feel at ease and many ask for him by name – at least the first or second time they call. Then, not so much.

Jared looks the part. The marketing division loves to feature him in promotional videos but he seems to be completely unaware of the value of other people's time. It's as if he has never used a calendar or planner in his life. He often misses calls and is frequently ill-prepared for meetings, although very skilled at winging it. At the same time, he is a deal-closer and, as such, brings value to his division.

Jared's boss has done a lot of reading on managing star talent and getting the most out of employees. Some of the readings suggest that employees can improve their reliability by being put in charge of others. Jared's boss wonders if this might be the case for Jared. There is a position coming up in the company which would mean a promotion for Jared, and a sales team to manage. It is a delicate time for the company as they are trying to establish a new market. Jared and his team would be the face of the company in this new market. Jared is likeable and talented but not reliable. He will probably leave if he doesn't get this promotion. Would you give him the promotion?

Your initial analysis (select all that apply)

☐ I would give him the promotion with a probationary period

☐ I would give him the promotion and ask him to take a course in time management

☐ I would not give him the promotion

☐ I would bring in an outsider for the promotion

☐ I would let the new team pick their own leader

Skillpod Insight

This is a tough one but here's our take – if Jared doesn't care about preparation and the value of other people's time, he is going to make a terrible manager of his team. He will set a bad example through his unreliability and multiply the incidence of poor performance throughout the division.

You can bet if Jared is unreliable at work, then his family and friends have been victims of this too. Those close to him have probably told him in clear terms that people who are unreliable and don't keep their word can't be trusted in relationships. The same is true in the workplace.

Until Jared learns to be a reliable person, he cannot help others prepare, perform or excel. He shouldn't lead.

TIPS | Having read this scenario, you will want to know how your family, friends and colleagues view your level of reliability. Go to the Toolbox at the end of the section and complete the Reliability Inventory. You can do this yourself or, if you are feeling brave, ask someone close to you to complete it for you. Otherwise, ask yourself the following questions:

- ▸ Would the people I most respect say that I keep my word?
- ▸ Do my friends trust me?
- ▸ Do I show up on time and ready for meetings, practices, classes and other commitments?
- ▸ Do people ask me for help?
- ▸ If I am late or let someone down, do I try to make it right?

Reflection:

Take a minute to reflect on a person on whom you can completely rely. How do you know that is the case? Write a few lines here.

DONE go back to your profile page and fill in a Selfwork block or
NOT YET continue to the next scenario or jump to the Toolbox at the end of the chapter for more practice.

SCENARIO 3
Visualizing a positive future

It was not a good time in Lea's life. Her courses were difficult, she was unhappy at work, she wasn't sleeping well and her lifestyle choices were not helping. These were all things she found difficult to discuss with family members. In her head, she couldn't move beyond thinking about what wasn't working in her life.

Her good friend, Ashley, saw that Lea was withdrawing and became concerned. Instead of asking, "What's wrong?", Ashley decided to ask a specific question, "How would your life look if you were happy?" She got Lea thinking about her future in really concrete ways – a year from now, how did she want to feel? How did she want to be spending her energy? Finally, what would success look like?

Once she started talking and imagining a future for herself, Lea became animated and engaged in the conversation. Together, Lea and Ashley drew a picture of a landscape which contained some challenging hills, a lovely river, peaceful meadows and rocky outcrops. Lea began the process of naming the steps she could imagine taking, how she would gather energy and financial resources to get her up the hills and over the outcrops, using swimming in the river and relaxing in the peaceful meadows to name activities that would give her life balance and bring her back to health. The metaphor of the landscape carried her thinking
to some imaginative places she would not have considered when she was feeling stuck.

At the end of one year, Lea's life had dramatically changed, and so had her priorities. On the one year anniversary, she and Ashley made the next map, this time using a graphic of the beautiful Gros Morne National Park, in Newfoundland, Canada, with its hiking trails, spectacular views, challenging climbs and unpredictable weather. She was feeling much more positive about herself and her choices and noticed the impact on her growing professional career which now had direction.

Your initial analysis (select all that apply)

☐ I think opportunities just present themselves and you have to be ready

☐ I find it difficult to believe that seeing myself succeeding will lead to success

☐ One of the hardest questions to answer is, "Where to do you want to go from this point and how will you get there?"

☐ I don't want to be where I am but I don't know where I want to go

☐ It's interesting to think that all aspects of my life and interests could be used to build a better future

Skillpod Insight

We are all at different places regarding to what extent envisioning a positive future can, in the language of Star Trek, "Make it so". In the list above, if you chose items one or two, you are right – opportunities do present themselves and it is challenging to make that leap from what is in your mind to what your life looks like. The fact that Lea had Ashley for a friend and that they were inspired to use drawing and metaphor to open up the conversation to possibility was key for them. Similar to the growth mindset information we provide in the module on Smarter Learning, having a positive and clear image of your future actually helps you to be alert to new opportunities and to see how emerging events can move you in the direction you want to go. If you chose items three or four, you see the challenge of forcing yourself to consider possible routes into the future and to assess how desirable or not are those routes.

Skillpod Insight

Rather than just letting life happen, you see the difficulty and the opportunity presented by thinking through your possible choices. If the fifth statement was one of your choices, you see the power of integrating all aspects of your life when you consider what directions best suit you. You must believe that you are in charge of your own destiny. This is not a life that is happening to you but one that you are creating.

TIPS | When considering your future path, start with identifying what success will look like for you – not for anyone else. Ask yourself these questions:

▸ Do I know what I need to accomplish in order to feel successful?

▸ Can I explain my goals to someone else? Have I done so?

▸ Have I analysed my goals to ensure I can be confident that that they will get me where I want to go?

▸ Can I anticipate what skills and knowledge I need to add to those I already have, and have I made a plan to achieve these?

▸ Who in my network can help and advise me?

Reflection:

Take a minute to imagine what you would draw if you were charting your future path. Describe or draw it here.

DONE go back to your profile page and fill in a Selfwork block or
NOT YET continue to the next scenario or jump to the Toolbox at the end of the chapter for more practice.

SCENARIO 4
Showing resilience

Before Ryan started his new job, he would have rated himself as a total self-starter. Throughout his college years, as a student, an athlete, a member of a band and a fitness buff, he had prided himself on his ability to set goals, keep focused on what was important, and gradually get better results in the things to which he was committed. He was a man in control and he liked how that felt.

The search for Ryan's job was a long one, with several disappointments. When his search was finally successful, Ryan was certain that the energy and motivation that had been so evident in his past endeavours would make him unstoppable. But in this new job, Ryan can barely get moving, let alone get traction. The learning curve at the company is steep and everyone else seems more competent and motivated than Ryan feels. He isn't used to that. He feels as if he is spinning his wheels.

A good friend of Ryan's suggests he find a coach who might be able to help him get back on track.

What do you think the coach will recommend?

Your initial analysis (select all that apply)

☐ Ryan should talk to his manager about his difficulties adjusting and ask for motivation

☐ Ryan should start looking for a job that is a better match for his skills and personality

☐ Ryan should begin to learn about his new company and to consider how he can add value to the enterprise

☐ Ryan should take a course in motivation

☐ Ryan should concentrate on his fitness and music interests and not rely so much on the job for life satisfaction

Skillpod Insight

Ryan has already learned two important facts. The first is that he is capable of sustained concentration that has led to success in a number of area. The second is that jobs are not easy to find. Fortunately, Ryan got some good advice from the coach, which was to harness all his past experience motivating himself in order to learn everything he can about how to become a motivated employee in this new job. Ryan has a lot to give but in these early days, he is a newbie. In order to regain the control that has helped motivate him in the past, Ryan needs the willpower and motivation to get through this period of feeling incompetent and to emerge from it as someone who can really contribute. He doesn't need a course, and he doesn't need to share with his boss that he is uncomfortable; he just needs to get on with making the situation at work a good one.

TIPS | Everything in this module on Selfwork comes down to these questions – can you build up your own character and experiences so that others will trust you? Can you envision how to succeed? Can you use motivation and willpower to get where you want to go? Willpower is what gets you through the discomfort and inconveniences you may experience – that feeling of incompetence, or frustration. Motivation is the urge to go forward – the future you can see or sense – that brass ring you are reaching for. You can activate both your willpower and motivation; both are completely within your control.

These hints may help:

► Try to anticipate avoidance tactics and devise a strategy to thwart procrastination.

► Tell someone else what you plan to do and by when – and set up your own penalty if you fail (make it hurt a little).

► Go into training – practise riding the discomfort wave – keep at an assignment for an hour longer than usual, stay at work an hour longer, ask for feedback on a project or your performance and challenge yourself to improve. All this helps build up resilience and willpower.

Reflection:

Resolve to stick at something just a little longer than is comfortable. Write down what you will try here. Write down how it felt.

DONE go back to your profile page and fill in a Selfwork block or
NOT YET continue to the next scenario or jump to the Toolbox at the end of the chapter for more practice.

Congratulations!

You have completed the Selfwork skill.

Self-Assessment:

Complete the following questions to assess your understanding of the material.

COMPETENCY		YES	NOT YET
1	I am able to control my reactions, temper and/or impulsiveness.		
1	My actions show that I have respect for others. The actions of others show that they have respect for me.		
2	I keep a planner or calendar and use it regularly.		
2	My family and friends know that they can count on me.		
3	I have an image of my future self that I keep in the front of my mind.		
3	I have long-range goals for myself.		
4	I have accomplished an important goal by using willpower.		
4	I have routines in my life that are linked to my goals.		

If you have answered **YES** to these questions, move on to the Selfwork portfolio entry page. If you have answered **NOT YET**, reflect on where you are running into roadblocks in your understanding of the related competency and what you can do to address this. Take a look a the Toolbox on the next page and try some of the exercises to deepen your understanding or mastery of the skill.

The Toolbox

Use the following activities to continue to build your Selfwork skills.

Self Control: (est. 25 seconds!)

When facing moments of panic, anger or embarrassment, close your eyes, breathe deeply and count to 25 before doing anything (that includes pressing "Send").

Reliability: (est. 10 min.)

Complete the following **Reliability Inventory**:

Score an **R** beside those items you think describe you and an **NR** where you think you are not reliable. Pick one item you gave an **NR**, and create a positive future statement. eg. "I will return things I have borrowed promptly." Read it over every day for a week.

You finish tasks on time . . . . .R . . . NR
You show up when you are supposed to. . . . . .R . . . NR
When you encounter obstacles, you work through them rather than giving up. . . . . .R . . . NR
You keep your promises . . . . .R . . . NR
Others know they can depend on you. . . . . .R . . . NR
You return things you have borrowed promptly. . . . . .R . . . NR
You always do your best.. . . . . .R . . . NR

Visualizing the future: (est. 30 min.)

Make a list of your top three past successes. Choose one and write five bullet points that summarize why and how you succeeded. Capture things like your state of mind at the time, the help or feedback you may have received, and the particular personal qualities that led to your success. The act of itemizing previous success provides concrete proof that you can succeed and puts you in a positive mindframe for upcoming challenges. Pick another success and do the exercise again. Do you see any patterns? Now, pick an upcoming challenge, close your eyes and imagine walking yourself through the experience with a positive mindset. Try to anticipate obstacles and your reactions. Finally, visualize successful completion of the task or challenge. Using your imagination in this way activates your powerful (and sometimes neglected) right brain.

Building motivation: (est. 1 hour)

When you have to get motivated to do a task you would rather not do (exercise, make a call you have been avoiding, complete your taxes), try to make it into a game of rewards and penalties – penalties are for procrastination and cost you one pleasurable activity (watching a game, playing, listening to music, screen time) for every minute you delay beginning. Rewards are quality points given for how completely and well you did the activity and entitle you to feel thoroughly virtuous!

Selfwork Portfolio Entry

You are ready to create a portfolio piece that captures your own unique Selfwork skill. Include skills-based language from the table below in your writing.

COMPETENCIES	ASSETS ("I...")
Valuing self and others	· am respected and respect others · have self control
Demonstrating reliability	· have good time management skills · am trusted
Visualizing a positive future	· can picture my future · have a life plan
Showing resilience	· have willpower · have helpful routines

STEP 1:

DEFINE
In your own words, define Selfwork.

What competencies are required for Selfwork?

STEP 1 (Continued):

DEMONSTRATE:
Using skills-based language, describe one specific experience that captures your skill in this area.

Where have you shown or used or observed these competencies in action?

ARTICULATE:
Why would an employer value your unique Selfwork skills?

STEP 2:

CREATE
Use the portfolio guidelines in the appendix to create a Selfwork portfolio entry.

STEP 3:

SHARE!
Feature this skill on your social media feed, your website, LinkedIn or online portfolio.

SKILL 3:
COMMUNICATION

The use of collaborative connections to share information in order to live, work and learn in the modern world.

Introduction

There has never been a time in history when communication was not important. The fundamental principles have not changed, particularly in face-to-face communication. However, there are lots more ways to communicate with each other, especially when the other person is not physically present. Not that long ago people communicated by the postal service and the telephone. What has happened since then is that communication has sped up globally and new channels for communication pop up (and disappear) at a dizzying pace. Personal networks grow very quickly and the management of these networks is a challenge. The boundaries between personal communication and private communication have been blurred, causing a loss of understanding of professional communication. At the same time, so much of communication has shifted to digital platforms that some interpersonal communication skills are also being lost. There are fundamentals to both interpersonal and digital communication, in both personal and professional realms, that need to be practised in order to improve.

Competencies:

1 Communicating your personal brand
Having an online presence is a standard practice both in professional and private realms and needs to be carefully managed.

2 Speaking and writing with authority
Use of correct grammar and language to articulate a clear, specific message and tailoring content to media and audience builds your credibility.

3 Listening actively
Listen with the goal of understanding others.

4 Creating persuasive presentations
Having a variety of presentation strategies (visual, spoken, written) allows you to match your communication style to the audience.

What employers value about strong Communication skills:

- ▸ Good digital citizenship
- ▸ Strong written skills (grammar and spelling, professional writing tone)
- ▸ Technical/creative skills (presentations, layout)
- ▸ Ability to speak to variety of audiences (internal, external)
- ▸ Confident presentation skills (verbal, visual)
- ▸ Attention to detail

What entrepreneurs value about strong Communication skills:

- ▸ Strong personal brand/clean digital footprint
- ▸ Persuasive presentations
- ▸ Robust network
- ▸ Adaptable communication style
- ▸ Ability to listen and absorb feedback

SCENARIO 1
Communicating your personal brand

Lucy Silver is an accomplished 28-year-old with a lifestyle YouTube channel that features celebrity fashion, diets and fitness routines and commands the attention of over 15,000 subscribers. Her "Lucyable" blog is also a popular guide to what's on locally. She is a sought-after speaker for schools and parent groups who see her as a role model for young women and she has made herself available on many occasions for these speaking engagements. Despite being a relative newcomer to town, it is no surprise to anyone when she is recruited to run in a local election and she is widely expected to win by a landslide.

Lucy's run for public office runs into trouble when a local journalist publishes a story about Lucy's high school years and her participation in a cyberbullying scandal focused on body-shaming her best friend, "because she wanted her (friend) to be the best she could be". Lucy was 17 at the time.

What would your next steps be if you were Lucy?

Your initial analysis (select all that apply)

☐ I would explain that it was a mistake I made 11 years ago, and I had learned from it

☐ I would hire a communications management firm to help me re-establish my good name

☐ I would interview my friend, who was my victim in high school, and who I knew had forgiven me and post the video

☐ I would let the bad press run its course and focus on the political campaign

☐ I would make a number of public statements taking ownership for my actions including an apology and an argument for why this early bad judgment should not define me

Skillpod Insight

You probably recognize Lucy's dilemma – it is similar to some we have seen in the news. It doesn't sound believable that you should be thinking about protecting your personal brand starting in your teenage years, but there are lots of examples of people whose professional and personal lives have been upended by the revelation of what they posted when they were in high school. And at 17, people pretty much think you are an adult. Given the situation, it doesn't really matter what steps you selected from the five above with respect to damage to Lucy's brand, but it does matter what Lucy does going forward. Her brand has been damaged and this is an opportunity to reforge an identify with some balance of empathy and inclusion to it, which we have deliberately left out of the description of her social media presence. Some combination of two and five above, as long as they are done in good faith and with integrity, are probably the best option.

There will be a story about your life, and if you don't tell it, someone else will. You need to have a storyline that highlights your strengths, your interests and what you want people to think about you – your values, your personal qualities. You need to keep private things private, using appropriate security to protect sensitive information. For public consumption (which is an audience that now includes potential employers, clients and other people who will want to know more about you), you need to show the side of you that benefits you and helps you achieve your career goals.

TIPS | Ask yourself these questions to get better at communicating your personal brand:

▶ Have I reviewed the privacy settings of my personal social media accounts?

▶ Do I have a set of posting rules for myself? Eg. never post in the heat of the moment, or when I am on an emotional roller-coaster?

▶ Do I protect my own reputation?

▶ Do I protect the reputations of others?

▶ Do I have the safeguards to avoid ever having to answer the question, "What were you thinking?" in reference to something I had posted on my own site or elsewhere?

Reflection:

Take a minute to reflect on a situation where you actively protected your personal brand or wish that you had. Write a few lines here.

DONE go back to your profile page and fill in a Communication block or
NOT YET continue to the next scenario or jump to the Toolbox at the end of the chapter for more practice.

SCENARIO 2
Speaking and writing with authority

Ari had a tough message to deliver. As the Senior Facilities Planner for a local university, it was his job to inform the tenants of a three block neighbourhood in the heart of the city, that the university would be reclaiming the neighbourhood for building purposes and would be relocating them elsewhere in the city. Some of the residents had lived in the area for over 15 years, some were elderly, and some had young children in local schools. Many were immigrants with varying levels of English proficiency. The level of disruption to their lives was immense. The university had already announced the decision in a press release, so when the neighbourhood meeting was called, the tenants knew what was in store, but not the details.

Ari's department had worked out the best compromise it could – the relocation would not occur for three years, the university would be providing housing in a pleasant neighbourhood with good schools 15 minutes away by public transit, and there would be advice and support during the transition period. Any tenant could vacate a lease without penalty at any time in the next three years if they preferred.

As an immigrant, Ari knew how fearful people could be of change, especially when there were some language issues. Every decision about his presentation to that meeting reflected his commitment to reassuring his audience that all would be OK, that they would be supported and their needs met. He carefully calculated what could best be presented by him, and what should transpire through conversation with others.

Ari posed five questions to himself that he felt were important to get right. How would you have answered?

Your initial analysis (select all that apply)

☐ Who is the audience? Who else could speak to the audience?

☐ Should he provide a summary of what would happen in the meeting at the start?

☐ What should be in the digital presentation he was offering?

☐ How should he think about the relationship of text to image in his presentation?

☐ To what extent should he provide information about the future plans for their neighbourhood?

Skillpod Insight

Communicating demands the careful consideration of context. Ari knew this. Here is what he finally decided:

He followed the famous advice of Cicero –" tell 'em what you're going to tell 'em". Especially in the case of delivering bad news, there should be no confusion about what information will be shared. In the introductory comments, Ari carefully explained the agenda for the meeting. Then, directly and without hesitation, he presented the issue and solution in a step-by-step manner in the introductory comments.

Ari invited people from the local schools to talk to families with young children. He also brought in representatives from neighbourhood organizations who could talk to people about access to new doctors, dentists, hairdressers, grocery stores – all the things that would be disrupted by the move to a new neighbourhood. He provided time in the second half of the meeting for people to join small discussion groups for the sharing of this information.

Skillpod Insight

Ari wanted his visual presentation to build a positive image of the new neighbourhood, so his preliminary slides focused on practical information – how people would get information about the move, what would happen during the next three years and who their contacts would be. This information was also in print and available on a website he had set up for the purpose. His presentation then moved on to visual images of the neighbourhood and plans and photos of the housing the university would provide.

Ari was aware that in his audience there was a mix of ages and ethnicity. He kept the slides visual and, where there was important text, he provided hard copy. His presentation was also on the website.

Ari made a second presentation, entirely separate from the first, which contained the plans for the new university buildings to be constructed in the neighbourhood. He decided he would offer the group the chance to see it, and those who wished, could stay. He also provided presentation as an audio download, a video and a Powerpoint on the website, to accommodate all learning styles.

TIPS | It is impossible to overstate the importance of accuracy in writing and speaking – using language that is grammatical, hitting the right tone and pitch for your audience, and getting the balance between text and image right. Challenge yourself to respond to these questions to improve your speaking and writing skills:

- ▶ Have I defined for myself what I want to accomplish with this communication?
- ▶ Have I done a thorough grammar and spelling check of my notes, slides and written documents?
- ▶ Do I know my audience? Have I pitched tone and language choices properly to appeal to them?
- ▶ Wherever possible, have I used images, charts or tables to make my information clearer and more memorable?
- ▶ Have I paid attention to the logic of my communication, so that listeners or readers will find it easy to grasp what I want them to know?

Reflection:

Take a minute to write about someone whose speaking and writing skills have impressed you. What does that kind of expertise convey to you?

DONE go back to your profile page and fill in a Communication block or
NOT YET continue to the next scenario or jump to the Toolbox at the end of the chapter for more practice.

SCENARIO 3
Listening actively

Frida was prepared. Her former employer had hired her to facilitate a session with some employees unhappy with a recent management decision. As an experienced facilitator, she knew the importance of planning ahead and as a former employee of her client, she knew those who would be at the meeting – some of them were her friends. She had planned a full program for the 90 minute meeting. Her client had briefed her on the organization's plan to rein in a part of the organization that considered itself autonomous – both in funding and in decision-making. The organization felt that it could achieve efficiencies if decision-making control were more centralized. The group knew why they had been called to a meeting and they weren't happy about it. Frida was concerned that there had been little consultation about the decision although, knowing the industry, she thought it was probably the right one. She anticipated a fairly rocky 90 minutes ahead.

Frida welcomed everyone and explained the purpose of the meeting, which was to build acceptance of the company's decision and to help the group work through the necessary changes. As she laid out the group assignments for the first information-gathering activity, one of Frida's former colleagues raised his hand and said he would first like the group to discuss the organization's decision, as it was counter to the group's interests, and to see if an argument could be made that the changes should not take place. He suggested hearing from everyone. There were 20 people at the meeting. All of them were nodding their heads in agreement.

Frida now has to decide on her next steps for the 90 minute meeting. She should:

Your initial analysis (select all that apply)

☐ Argue in favour of the organization's decision, remind the group it is not their decision to make, and move on with her plan

☐ Turn the meeting over to the senior manager attending the meeting and step aside

☐ Suggest that she consolidate 2 of the planned activities, thereby freeing up 20 minutes that could be allocated to 5 speakers who would speak for the group

☐ Revamp the first activity so that it becomes a group opportunity to collect feedback about why the plan is a bad idea

☐ Ask for a 5 minute break, consult with the manager in confidence, and propose that she become the facilitator for the group so that their dissent could be voiced

Skillpod Insight

We should all wish never to be in Frida's shoes! This scenario has all the elements that would most greatly test even the best communicator. Frida has to walk a fine line. If she is overly formal or overly informal with her former colleagues, she will lose credibility. If she doesn't control the time, the entire 90 minutes will turn into a grievance session without a positive outcome, and she will have made the situation worse. But if she doesn't turn the session into an opportunity for the employees to have a voice, the organization will be dealing with a very negative group going forward.

Frida thinks about and rejects the first two options above. She is a facilitator not a spokesperson for the company, but she has been hired to do a job and she must do her best.

Skillpod Insight

She thinks hard about the third option, but realizes the time needed to select the 5 people and allow them to prepare a few comments will erode the 20 minutes allocated and the speaker will get a scant 2 minutes at most to speak which will only aggrieve the employees even more. Frida selects a combination of options four and five. She uses the groups she has already assigned and changes the activity to one in which each group lists two pros and two cons of the planned reorganization and one alternative to it. While they are busy, she confers with the senior manager, and suggests they conduct a feedback session for the group, with an end goal of giving the people affected by the decision both a voice and an opportunity to suggest alternative steps, should they wish to do so.

TIPS | Even the brightest lights among us can wind up in the dark about the importance of listening. Most of us are far too preoccupied with ourselves and what we have to say and pay too little attention to what others want to communicate to us. Never is this more of a risk than when you are leading a group discussion, making a presentation or facilitating a discussion, especially when the stakes are high. Active listening must be practised to be learned. Remind yourself of these techniques when it is important that you hear as well as speak!

Ask yourself these questions to get better at active listening:

▸ Do I know what others are hoping to get out of the session? Have I asked?

▸ Have I planned for feedback during the meeting or session? What will I do with that feedback? How will I gather it?

▸ Have I used research at appropriate times to build confidence in my listeners?

▸ Have I published objective criteria to help others evaluate the ideas and frame questions?

▸ Am I prepared to openly accept the feedback that I am asking for?

Reflection:

Take a minute to reflect on a situation where you have seen someone manage a situation that straddles professional and personal boundaries by listening actively. How did they do it and why was it effective? Write a few lines here.

DONE go back to your profile page and fill in a Communication block or
NOT YET continue to the next scenario or jump to the Toolbox at the end of the chapter for more practice.

SCENARIO 4
Creating persuasive presentations

Bill and Jojo have a startup called 'Lightbox' that uses a teleconferencing platform to build online communities. Their audience are people who, for a variety of reasons, are limited in their ability to move about – new mothers, seniors, those with chronic conditions, caregivers and those living in isolated rural areas, to name a few. People "shop" for groups with expertise or interests similar to their own and focus on working together on projects. The site provides instruction, connections, games and information.

They know their idea is replicable and scalable across many jurisdictions. They need to raise a significant amount of money in order to develop their interface for such a variety of needs, test their prototype in a variety of markets and get feedback from users.

Their idea is appealing to a number of funding sources, one of which is a group of 100 people who each give $4000 per annum to build a fund, the full amount of which is awarded to a project considered to be of most benefit to the community it targets and best positioned to take advantage of a $400k injection of capital. To enter the competition, each project must submit detailed financials in a business plan and a working prototype of the web app. Five projects will be selected for the presentation round. Bill and Jojo's project makes the cut and moves on in the competition. The rules of the competition round are simple – a visual presentation of no more than seven minutes with no Q&A, before an audience of 7-15 people whose backgrounds and profiles will not be revealed. Up to 10 pages of supplementary material may be provided. The location is a hotel meeting room. There will be a run off between the two top finishers. Bill and Jojo have a week to prepare.

How should Jojo and Bill spend their seven minutes?

Your initial analysis (select all that apply)

☐ Their presentation should be equally divided between proving the benefits of the idea and their suitability to make best use of the money

☐ Their presentation should provide profiles of potential users and an explanation of the interface they hope to develop

☐ They should spend a minute on each of the following: the problem the idea will address, the solution the idea will offer, the metrics that will demonstrate success, potential competitors and potential users

☐ They should present a case for solving the problems of isolation and lack of stimulation, and focus on the positive outcomes for the individuals who will benefit

☐ They should provide testimonials from both users and their caregivers

Skillpod Insight

Jojo and Bill determine that as they have already provided detailed financial information, they can use the supplementary information package as an opportunity to highlight the need, the benefits, the stability and capacity of their organization and their business model. They will be sure the package has been distributed before their presentation begins and refer to it during the presentation. They design a presentation, including short but high impact stories, with the goal of building empathy in the audience for the isolated population they are trying to help. They make effective use of visual images to illustrate the challenges facing the end users and their caregivers, and the benefits to them as their worlds begin to open up.

TIPS | To be truly persuasive, you have to engage the attention and curiosity of your audience. Ask yourself these questions to get better at making a persuasive presentation:

- ▶ Have I clearly stated the problem and the solution?
- ▶ Have I made an emotional connection with the audience?
- ▶ Have I used the best evidence to support my argument?
- ▶ Have I used pictures and stories to engage the imagination?
- ▶ Have I ensured my vocabulary is free from jargon and "insider" language?
- ▶ Does my presentation help the audience to answer the questions, "Who will benefit?" and "Why should I care?"?

Reflection:

What is the most persuasive argument/presentation you have ever heard? Why were you persuaded? Write a few lines here.

DONE go back to your profile page and fill in a Communication block or
NOT YET continue to the next scenario or jump to the Toolbox at the end of the chapter for more practice.

Congratulations!

You have completed the Communication skill.

Self-Assessment:

Complete the following questions to assess your understanding of the material.

	COMPETENCY	YES	NOT YET
1	I believe that managing my online presence matters to my future.		
1	I am careful about what I share online.		
2	I am confident that in speaking and writing I use the correct tone and language for my audience.		
2	I understand that communication includes accurate written and visual material.		
3	I ask a question to look for clarity before reacting to a statement that I don't agree with.		
3	I work at ensuring all my communications involve both sharing information and listening to others.		
4	I have a variety of strategies to engage my listeners.		
4	I know how to match my communication style to my audience.		

If you have answered **YES** to these questions, move on to the Communication portfolio entry page. If you have answered **NOT YET,** reflect on where you are running into roadblocks in your understanding of the related competency and what you can do to address this. Take a look a the Toolbox on the next page and try some of the exercises to deepen your understanding or mastery of the skill.

The Toolbox

Use the following activities to dig deeper and continue to build your Communication skills.

Matching media/mode to audience: (est. 30 min.)

You are a fundraiser for a rural charity whose work is focused on the two ends of the spectrum, youth and seniors. Your job is to design the materials for the annual fundraising drive in support of their organization. The goal is to double the amount raised last year. You think that means you will need to reach at least three times the number of people. The most supportive people in the community so far have been young people who have done the bulk of the volunteer work, and a prosperous group of retirees who have given generously.

You have social media, a website, radio and TV spots and a news magazine interview all lined up. On a piece of paper, create three columns. List all the media in the left column. Match each of these media to the audience you would target with that media in the middle column. Finally, in the right hand column list in one sentence the key message for each media, tailoring these messages to the specific audience.

Distinguishing personal from professional communication: (est. 1 hour)

You have a great idea for a local car sharing business. You want to pilot it with your friends first, to work out the bugs, and then to try to sell the idea to a group of local investors.

Write a paragraph introducing your idea to each of these two groups, with a view to making your friends want to participate and investors to fund the project.

Listening: (est. 5 min.)

Note: This exercise requires two people. Listening is much more challenging that it seems. Try this quick exercise with a partner. Sit in chairs facing each other. One person will tell a story for 60 seconds. The goal for the second person is to do whatever they can to not listen: look at your phone, sing, walk around, do not make eye contact. If you are talking, your goal is to keep talking no matter what, even if you have to follow the other person around, talk louder, etc. Stop at 60 seconds and have each person share the experience of not listening and not being heard. Write yourself three tips for listening more effectively the next time someone talks to you.

Using appropriate tone: (est. 1 hour)

There is more to effective communication than just words. Voice, body language and visual imagery all play important roles in creating the appropriate tone for the communication. Recognizing this is key to getting it right. Your exercise is to find one situation, maybe from the news, a professional meeting or personal experience, in which the tone and content of what someone was trying to communicate was off and one that was dead on. One might be quite funny and some appalling. Make a five point list of what made one effective and one miss the mark. How would you go about deciding on tone for your next presentation?

Communication Portfolio Entry

You are ready to create a portfolio piece that captures your own unique Communication skill. Include skills-based language from the table below in your writing.

COMPETENCIES	ASSETS ("I...")
Communicating your personal brand	· manage my online presence · am deliberate about what I share online
Speaking and writing with authority	· tailor my tone to the content and audience · create accurate written and visual material
Listening actively	· seek understanding · communicate by listening and sharing
Creating persuasive presentations	· have strategies to engage audience · use appropriate media/modes

STEP 1:

DEFINE
In your own words, define Communication.skills.

STEP 1 (Continued):

DEMONSTRATE:
Using skills-based language, describe one specific experience that captures your skill in this area.

ARTICULATE:
Why would an employer value your unique Communication skills?

Think about this from an employer's perspective.

STEP 2:

CREATE
Use the portfolio guidelines in the appendix to create a Communication portfolio entry.

STEP 3:

SHARE!
Feature this skill on your social media feed, your website, LinkedIn or online portfolio.

SKILL 4:
TEAMWORK

The means of reaching a goal through collaboration that is not achievable by an individual alone.

Introduction

Collaboration can take many forms. It can be loose and informal, whereas teamwork generally has more structure and is characterized by the purpose of people coming together in order to meet a goal that can't be met by an individual.

We think of teamwork mainly in terms of sports. In sports, it is easy to see that successful teams are those whose members collaborate well while achieving their goal. However, professionally, people often work in teams as well.

Employers often state that they are looking for good "team-players". If you have never been an athlete, this may be intimidating or unclear. A good team-player understands the various roles on the team, clearly understands the goal and knows that they cannot achieve this goal alone. Understanding team roles, and tailoring conditions to each situation is at the heart of understanding team work.

Competencies:

1 Working with integrity
The work of others is always acknowledged.
Support your teammates.

2 Understanding team roles and operational norms
In effective teams, there is a team leader and members have clear roles. Ground rules or "norms" are discussed and established.

3 Clarifying team goals
The first job of the team is to clearly define the objective they are trying to achieve.

4 Critically evaluating the outcome
Successful teams clearly define what success will look like, gather data throughout the process and evaluate it at the end of the project.

What employers value about strong Teamwork skills:

- ▸ Flexibility, adaptability
- ▸ Works with integrity
- ▸ Commitment to team goals
- ▸ Values perspectives of others
- ▸ Positive attitude, sense of humour
- ▸ Manages conflict objectively
- ▸ Experience collaborating

What entrepreneurs value about strong Teamwork skills:

- ▸ Ability to manage conflict
- ▸ Team leadership
- ▸ Integrity
- ▸ Willingness to take on any role
- ▸ Ability to work with a variety of people
- ▸ Commitment to team goals

SCENARIO 1
Working with integrity

Amy had a major project given to her by her firm. It was complex and international in scope, and, of course, there was a tight deadline. Her first challenge was to create a team to provide the best outcome in the given time, (always less than imagined)! She did think of just doing it herself – believing deep down that it is always the fastest way – but realized that there were some key things she absolutely needed from others and there was no way she could complete this project alone in the time frame provided.

Amy took on the work of design, research and prototyping. However, she needed support in the areas of communications and organizational planning. She found Toan for the organizational work and

Nikki for communications. Toan was a very talented workaholic who produced a professional organizational plan and gave it to Nikki to put into an attractive format for a presentation. Nikki completed her task and presented the work but took the entire credit for the project, failing to acknowledge that the organizational plan was Toan's work and the rest of it was Amy's. Toan was deeply offended. As a result, the professional relationship between Toan and Nikki was broken. While Amy was not particularly bothered by having her work usurped by someone else, she did realize that trust among the three of them had been broken and that the team had ceased to function effectively.

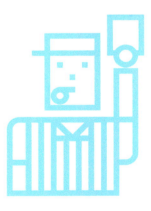

Your initial analysis (select all that apply)

☐ Toan was a bad choice for the team

☐ Amy did not understand how good teams worked

☐ Nikki let Amy down

☐ The structure of the team was inadequate

☐ Amy should have acknowledged Nikki's lack of integrity

Skillpod Insight

Integrity is a key and common issue in working with others. Unfortunately some people just see the world as owing them and claim much more credit than is due. The resentment built up by this can ruin very good projects. Nikki is an example of this. Amy's lack of action makes things worse. It was Amy's responsibility to preserve the operating values of the team and to ensure people work in a safe, trusting environment. Unfortunately the lack of integrity is very common when stakes are high. Never bad-mouth or gossip about another teammate. The important element of trust is built when teammates know they can count on each other and when they see others acting with integrity.

TIPS | Ask yourself these questions to get better at working with integrity:

- ▶ Do I commit to the team's values, norms, plans and priorities?
- ▶ Do I commit to the role that is needed or given to me and respect the roles of others?
- ▶ Do I avoid gossip and work to resolve conflict in a healthy manner as it arises?
- ▶ Am I ready to jump in and help a teammate who is struggling?
- ▶ Do I bring a positive attitude to the teamwork despite challenges or bumps in the road?
- ▶ Do I acknowledge the contributions of others?

Reflection:

Take a minute to reflect on a situation in which someone claimed credit for work not their own. Write a few lines here.

DONE go back to your profile page and fill in a Teamwork block or
NOT YET continue to the next scenario or jump to the Toolbox at the end of the chapter for more practice.

SCENARIO 2
Understanding team roles and operational norms

Siona was instructed to build a team to address a challenging problem her company faced. As with many of these challenges, new market conditions and the digital impact on operations were front and centre. Siona needed a strong team that included expertise in the business, the latest technological advances, and importantly, with good team attitude. Siona had a few close colleagues that she added to her team. George, an IT expert, joined and recommended a couple of his colleagues. Siona had her group including a communications and services expert. All members were very positive about the challenge, and they took up their work enthusiastically. Because they were all experienced professionals, Siona assumed they did not need much managing, assigned tasks to various people and and left them to get on with it.

After a few weeks at a check in meeting, Siona found that the various elements of the project were coming along but that there was incredible tension among the members. George and his group made a terrific visual presentation that overshadowed the work of the communication person Siona brought in. One from Siona's group made a proposal for IT changes that would mean more work for George's group. As a result, George and his group began to develop new norms of working which included different working hours, and a different workspace and conducting meetings just for their group.

Siona was left with half a team that worked to the original terms, and the other half whose members had effectively created their own team with their own rules. None of them were respecting boundaries of their disciplines, nor were they respecting Siona's leadership. Siona was left with the very tough realization that she had lost control of the situation and that the project was in danger of not meeting its targets. How would she save the project?

Your initial analysis (select all that apply)

☐ Both groups were acting properly and taking advantage of ideas that they were generating

☐ George was disrespecting Siona's role as a team leader

☐ Siona was a bad team leader

☐ Siona was a good team leader because she let people do what they wanted

☐ The roles and operational norms were not established well enough

Skillpod Insight

Roles and norms are important for a team to succeed. This is especially true for groups where members are new to each other and where there is no history of trust. Roles can be divided according to expertise (research, communications, finance, etc) or by task. Occasionally, you will be asked to do something or will need to do something outside of your expertise. Flexibility and good attitude and a willingness to do what needs to be done will help contribute to a group's success. If you are heading outside your agreed-to role, be mindful that you are not stepping on other people's toes. In the scenario above, Siona had not established the roles or operating norms clearly enough. George did not play his role in supporting Siona. His whole group followed his lead. As in sports, teammates who decide to play a different position on the field, or change the rules as they play, throw the team into chaos and distract the group from achieving the goal.

TIPS | Ask yourself these questions to get better at understanding team roles and operating norms:

- ► Have the team values, operating norms and goals been discussed and agreed on by all members?
- ► Are the essential team roles (functional or expertise-based) identified and covered?
- ► Does the team have a process for handling disagreements and conflict?
- ► Have I considered the team members' PLP to ensure complementary and diverse viewpoints are represented?
- ► Can I play any role that is asked of me even if it is outside my comfort zone?

Reflection:

If you were Siona, how would you save this situation and get the project back on track? Write a few lines here.

DONE (go back to your profile page and fill in a Teamwork block) or
NOT YET (continue to the next scenario or jump to the Toolbox at the end of the chapter for more practice).

Clarifying team goals

The town of Burnside was thrilled when Glen, a former hockey player in the regional league, volunteered to be the coach of the local girls' hockey team. Although he had no coaching experience, everyone assumed he would raise the girls' game. But as someone new to coaching, he mistakenly assumed that the girls would all be at comparable skill levels. It never occurred to him that varying skill levels and reasons for being on the team could so complicate the coaching requirements. He also assumed that decisions about the team were entirely his call.

Take, for example, Kate and Joyce. Kate, who was a naturally gifted player, had an ambitious mother, Sophie. Sophie expected Kate to eventually qualify for a Varsity level team. Jim's daughter, Joyce, who was shy and lacked self-confidence, was there to have a team experience and to build her confidence. Jim believed that playing on a local team with her many friends would be just the thing to help her grow.

Glen was a competitive guy. As the season progressed, it became more and more apparent to the parents that Glen's goal was to win the league title. They did not feel part of this decision. While Glen did have some parental support, and the team did well, it meant that some girls had much more ice time than others and many parents objected. Kate was a star and played on the first line

and the special teams. Joyce was on the fourth line and saw little ice time. Her self-confidence, instead of growing, plummeted. The rest of the team felt badly for Joyce – a genuinely kind person, whom they all liked. They wanted her to have the ice time and worked with her to improve her skills. Conflict among the girls and their parents began to emerge.

Sophie, Kate's mom, said players like Joyce should find a league more suited to their abilities.

Glen said his job was to coach, not to deal with relationship problems. Jim, Joyce's dad, arranged a meeting of the parents to discuss next steps.

Your initial analysis (select all that apply)

☐ Jim was out of line calling the meeting

☐ Glen was out of touch with the parents' priorities

☐ The girls should have had more say in the process

☐ It was unclear what the goals of the team were

☐ The main players were not communicating with each other

Skillpod Insight

This scenario is a classic case of a team starting their season (or a project) with ill-defined goals. There were several options that should have been clear from the start. Was the goal for the season to have every girl play more or less equal time? Or was the goal to win the league? Or was the goal just to maximize fun and learn some skills along the way? Each option changes the strategy and the goal for the season. In the workplace time and money are wasted if goals are not crystal clear, well communicated and agreed to by the whole team.

TIPS | Ask yourself these questions to get better at helping teams clarify goals:

- ▶ Has the team identified clear team goals?
- ▶ Have they been discussed and agreed to by all members of the group?
- ▶ Is there a clear plan in place for how to achieve the goals and monitor progress?
- ▶ Can I support ways of achieving team goals that seem radically different from the ways I would have chosen?
- ▶ Are all team members encouraged to communicate their thoughts?
- ▶ What role does communication play in the exercise?

Reflection:

Take a minute to reflect on a situation you have encountered in which team goals were (or were not) clear. Write a few lines here.

DONE go back to your profile page and fill in a Teamwork block or
NOT YET continue to the next scenario or jump to the Toolbox at the end of the chapter for more practice.

SCENARIO 4
Critically evaluating the outcome

Outcomes are the result of actions. At times, outcomes may or may not meet our anticipated goals. One important concept of reaching goals as a team is critically evaluating unintended outcomes.

Dev had a plan to create an organization to help underprivileged youth. His anticipated goal was to help at least 20 youth gain admission to college. He found four young talented people to help him, many of whom had grown up in neighbourhoods similar to the one which he had chosen for his project. He designed a program to address literacy, numeracy and a number of soft skills and secured funding for it. The program opened with lots of optimism but, very soon, unexpected difficulties arose. The youth in the program had little support from home to attend and so after the first few days, attendance deteriorated. One of Dev's employees explained that by using an old school for the site, the message to the youth was that this was "school" and many soon were turned off. In addition, the neighbourhood was tough and there were a number of acts of vandalism and theft that were discouraging for the team. The team worked bravely to overcome obstacles and redesign the program, but gradually the enterprise withered. The end of year "graduation" was dispiriting with only a third of the expected students completing the program.

In the debrief to evaluate the program, Dev and his team realized that the underprivileged youth faced many negative circumstances that the program had not addressed, but which made it difficult to succeed. As discouraging as this was, Dev's team realized that they had clear, collective vision of success. They were able to collect data through the input of all team members during the program. In the evaluation and analysis they realized that although they had a good team with the right balance of skills, that there were factors beyond their understanding that had prevented the program's success. This was a good learning experience for the team but now they need to write the funding report. What will Dev say to the donors?

Your initial analysis (select all that apply)

☐ Dev could have better managed the team

☐ The team had no common vision of success

☐ The project was as successful as it could have been

☐ There were important learnings that can be applied to a future program both from a team perspective and a project perspective

☐ Failure is an acceptable outcome as long as you learn from it

---

Skillpod Insight

Sometimes, even if the collective vision is clear, there are unpredictable factors that throw off success. In this case, Dev had collected a great team with diverse skills and clearly outlined roles and organizational norms. They had collectively established a clear vision of success and had created a process for collecting data along the way. However, Dev's team was hit with a case of group myopia. They saw the future that they wanted to see. It takes a brave team leader to critically evaluate an unsuccessful outcome, to take responsibility for the team's work and to identify insights from learnings that can be applied in future team projects. The skill of critically evaluating an outcome can be applied to both team projects and non-team projects.

TIPS | Remind yourself these points and questions to get better at critically evaluating outcomes:

- ▶ Have I anticipated a range of possible outcomes, both good and bad?
- ▶ Am I confident of the steps for critical analysis of outcomes (anticipate, plan, collect feedback/data, analyse, learn/share)?
- ▶ Have I establish data that can be collected during the project to help with the evaluation of the outcomes?
- ▶ Do I have an evaluation model for the project?
- ▶ Can I frame a failed attempt as a learning opportunity?

Reflection:

Take a minute to reflect on a team project that was not successful. Was there a critical evaluation process built into the planning? If so, what was learned from the final evaluation? If not, why not? Write a few lines here.

DONE go back to your profile page and fill in a Teamwork block or
NOT YET continue to the next scenario or jump to the Toolbox at the end of the chapter for more practice.

Congratulations!

You have completed the Teamwork skill.

Self-Assessment:

Complete the following questions to assess your understanding of the material.

	COMPETENCY	YES	NOT YET
1	I acknowledge the work of others.		
1	I work hard to follow the team's organizational plans and priorities.		
2	I can play various roles in a team as needed.		
2	I know how to work through conflict.		
3	I commit to team goals and staying on track.		
3	I try to be positive with competing ideas.		
4	I take time to critically evaluate the success of completed project.		
4	I focus on learning from each team experience.		

If you have answered **YES** to these questions, move on to the Teamwork portfolio entry page. If you have answered **NOT YET,** reflect on where you are running into roadblocks in your understanding of the related competency and what you can do to address this. Take a look at the Toolbox on the next page and try some of the exercises to deepen your understanding or mastery of the skill.

The Toolbox

Use the following activities to dig deeper and continue to build your Teamwork skills.

Acknowledging the work of others: (15 min.)

Common examples of lack of integrity on a team include using others' work as your own and/or failing to acknowledge the work of others. How to test this? Since you do not want to ruin a team by practising the theft of others' work, try the observation route. Take one team you are on or have been on recently. Get a piece of paper and and set out the roles and contributions each member has made. Track whether any members acknowledged the work of other members. Think about your own work on teams. Write out one opportunity you had to acknowledge the work of others. Did you do it? If not, why not? Commit to doing this in your next team project and make note of the reaction. Acknowledging people's contributions is a great leadership technique.

Committing to team goals and staying on track: (30 min.)

The whole point of a team is to achieve a goal. A team composed of members with different or conflicting goals cannot succeed. We see that all over the place. Even when all agree on the goal, many will have different ways to get there. Staying on track is crucial. So think of a team you are or were on and assess two things: first, were all members committed to the same goal, and second, did they have a good plan to stay focussed in reaching the goal effectively. What can you learn from this experience?

Acting on informed feedback: (1 hour total)

We see all sorts of important actions that act against informed feedback. Do we act on what we want to believe, or do we act on informed feedback? And what if informed feedback opposes what we want to do or write about? Think of a situations where you have not used the best feedback for an important action and the result was a poor decision. Why didn't you use the best feedback – did you ignore it? How would things have been different had you acted upon that feedback? Outline the reasons for your actions and how things would be different had you listened more carefully to the feedback you ignored. What three tips would you give someone else to encourage them to listen more carefully to the feedback?

Dealing with conflict: (30 min.)

Conflict is universal. It will never disappear but in most situations it can be managed. Some conflict is not a bad thing. It represents differing viewpoints which can be a great source of creativity. Sometimes we need to agree to disagree. However, in very tense situations, you can actively manage or deescalate the situation by being prepared. Think about one example of a team where members were in conflict. What was the outcome? Check these factors that could have helped. Was there a calm and mature team leader? Did every member have a say regarding the issues? Was there agreement on the goals and means of achieving them? Do you think that this list could have helped the situation you are thinking about? If yes, great! If not, what else might have helped?

Teamwork Portfolio Entry

You are ready to create a portfolio piece that captures your own unique Teamwork skill. Include skills-based language from the table below in your writing.

COMPETENCIES	ASSETS ("I...")
Working with integrity	· acknowledge the work of others · respect team's organizational plan and priorities
Understanding roles and norms	· can play various team roles · can manage conflicts
Clarifying team goals	· commit to team goals · understand competing goals
Critically evaluating outcomes	· commit to evaluating success · learn from team experience

STEP 1:

DEFINE
In your own words, define Teamwork skills.

STEP 1 (Continued):

DEMONSTRATE:
Using skills-based language, describe one specific experience that captures your skill in this area.

ARTICULATE:
Why would an employer value your unique Teamwork skills?

STEP 2:

CREATE
Use the portfolio guidelines in the appendix to create a Teamwork portfolio entry.

STEP 3:

SHARE!
Feature this skill on your social media feed, your website, LinkedIn or online portfolio.

SKILL 5:
INFORMATION
MANAGEMENT

Information management is the collection and management of information from one or more sources, and its distribution to one or more sources.

Introduction

In a world of information overload it is becoming increasingly important to have systems and strategies, "life hacks" as it were, to manage information in your life and not have it manage you. There are two areas that are worth monitoring: information that you knowingly or unknowingly invite into your world and information you knowingly or unknowingly send out into the world.

Our world is increasingly dominated by word-of-mouth information sources, or by sources that have very one-dimensional views. This means each of us must go out of our way to ensure that the information that we draw from represents diversity of views and is based on fact rather than opinion and assumptions. Equally important is managing what we are putting out into the world, and understanding that there is little distinction between our private and professional worlds.

Competencies:

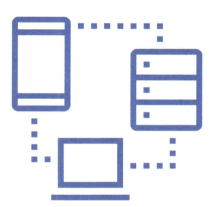

1 Choosing good sources
The importance of drawing information from a range of documented, reliable sources that express a range of biases.

2 Storing and retrieving of information
Applying a personal system for managing vast amounts of information given the fast changing nature of platforms and media formats.

3 Understanding usefulness of data
Understanding how and why organizations gather and manage "big data".

4 Valuing digital privacy
Taking action to protecting your personal information as well as that of others.

What employers value about strong Information Management skills:

- ▶ Critical thinking
- ▶ Organization/ technical skills
- ▶ Good systems thinking
- ▶ Excellent discrimination skills
- ▶ Understanding of privacy (and confidentiality)

What entrepreneurs value about strong Information Management skills:

- ▶ Efficiency
- ▶ Systems
- ▶ Correct information
- ▶ Organization
- ▶ Privacy (and confidentiality)

Choosing good sources

Lizzie and Simone were successful candidates for two research jobs advertised by their life coach, who was producing a new video series for his YouTube channel. The videos addressed the stresses of living in a fast-paced world and were meant to offer information about healthy choices in areas like finances, nutrition, work-life balance and exercise. The goal of the videos was to deliver soft but accurate information that would help people without intimidating them and, of course, to generate some business for the coach.

Lizzie, as a business student, saw this opportunity as a way to drive participants to the website of the life coach and to increase his practice. She therefore favoured sources that reinforced the beliefs the coach already had about these topics, even though some of his sources were dated. She thought it was important that the information in the videos and on the website aligned perfectly.

Simone was a history major. Her approach to the research was to locate the most current research and to follow up closely in cases where there seemed to be conflicting advice on the video topics. And, especially in fields like nutrition and exercise, she found that thinking had shifted pretty dramatically in the last ten years about balanced eating and exercise and that even in some of the most current research there remained sharp disagreements.

The two researchers presented their information which was, in some cases, significantly different. The coach had some decisions to make.

Your initial analysis (select all that apply)

☐ Older information isn't necessarily less accurate than newer

☐ The business priorities should be dominant – that was the purpose of the series and besides, no one really cares that much about what other experts might say

☐ The coach should have made the criteria for selecting sources clearer

☐ To present all points of view would weaken the value of the coach's advice

☐ The coach's beliefs should form the basis of the information presented in the series

Skillpod Insight

Reflecting for a moment on our earlier module on Selfwork, we know that if people do not consider a person to be reliable, they cannot trust either that person or the information he might provide. Although Lizzie was in tune with the coach's business aspirations, and probably had the skills to advance the business case through the video series, she did him no favours by selecting only information that confirmed existing advice, while ignoring information that was more current and perhaps more reliable. It's not that older information is always less accurate – it's just that looking at the most current research on a topic, especially from a reliable source, provides a better sense of how people's understanding of a topic may have developed. By using Simone's research, the coach would be able to provide a richer picture of the best thinking on some of these topics. His potential clients, therefore, would benefit – which makes great business sense as well being the right thing to do.

TIPS | Ask yourself these questions to get better at selecting good sources:

- ▸ Is my information from current and reputable sources?
- ▸ Are my sources in-depth and based on fact rather than opinion? How do I know?
- ▸ Can I find corroborating evidence from another reliable source?
- ▸ Is my information relevant to the topic I am researching?
- ▸ Do my sources acknowledge other points of view?

Reflection:

Take a minute to reflect on a situation in which you could have used better sources of information than you did. Write a few lines here.

DONE go back to your profile page and fill in a Information Management block or
NOT YET continue to the next scenario or jump to the Toolbox at the end of the chapter for more practice.

SCENARIO 2
Storing and retrieving of information

Jules is a strategy consultant who thinks in terms of what might work well in the future. Her preoccupation is in imagining an outcome that produces real benefits to others. She is very convincing when explaining these things to others and they want to help. She has gathered a great team around her to help realize her new project. She will have to work with her editing and media team to create a persuasive presentation and a prototype of the web-based approach she is proposing.

To get things started, Jules wrote a promotional document and then used simple software to build a model website to show what she was thinking. She thought it looked good. She shared a text copy document with one colleague, Ana, who was a good, efficient editor. Ana made her revisions and comments and sent the text back to Jules immediately. Jules saved the file to review later. But by the time she got to it, Jules's thinking had moved on and so she made some new additions and sent them back to Ana without completing the first set of revisions. Ana found more errors in the new material and highlighted some revisions Jules had failed to make in the first round, sending the material back to Jules. Jules misfiled the most recent version from Ana and wound up replying to the older version, asking why the latest changes had not been incorporated. Ana exploded in frustration.

Yoni was Jules's media expert, and was ultimately responsible for the website component. He saw the prototype of the site she had made and asked for the files so he could continue the work. Yoni had a similar experience with Jules. She either couldn't find files and asked they be resent, or she worked on older versions, causing people to redo work they had already completed. Miscommunication and lack of attention to detail caused huge problems and stress throughout the team and project delays.

Your initial analysis (select all that apply)

- ☐ Jules should have been much more aware of the editing process

- ☐ Ana should have identified Jules's issues with sorting and retrieving files and provided her with a solution

- ☐ Everyone on the team should have had a clear idea as to how the files would be identified

- ☐ Jules should have allowed Yoni to create the website from the start

- ☐ Jules omitted step one: to ensure that everyone was on the same page in the process

Skillpod Insight

The two main issues in this scenario are the management and sharing of media and the need for a good storage system. Jules lacked both. Despite the fact that her team got her through, she gave up significant goodwill in the process. That cost her both time and return on any investment she made. A thoughtful and consistent system of file nomenclature and storage is a strategic advantage for a team. An active person might generate several dozen new files of various kinds in a day. It is better to spend some time in the early stages of a project organizing a system of file naming and a file framework, or deciding on a file sharing platform that allows teams to access the relevant information quickly and accurately. Finally, Once a project is complete, there should be a final culling and organization of files so that they can be easily retrieved if ever needed. No one wants to be searching endlessly for files!

TIPS | Ask yourself these questions to get better at information storage and retrieval:

- ▶ Have I established a system for naming files and creating folders/tagging?
- ▶ When working with a team, have I agreed to shared file protocols such as naming and file creation?
- ▶ Do I separate the final version of a document, by location and naming, from the previous draft versions?
- ▶ If someone were to take over a project from me, could they easily follow my filing logic and access critical information easily?
- ▶ Do I rename documents and pictures from other sources in order to make them conform to my filing logic?

Reflection:

Take a minute to reflect on a situation where not naming or organizing files properly had a negative outcome, and what you could have done differently. Write a few lines here.

DONE go back to your profile page and fill in a Information Management block or
NOT YET continue to the next scenario or jump to the Toolbox at the end of the chapter for more practice.

SCENARIO 3
Understanding the usefulness of data

Although we think of data management as a factor of our digital era, our example here comes from a historic episode of data gathering and analysis. In London, UK in 1853, 616 people died from a cholera outbreak. The outbreak was mostly restricted to one neighbourhood. At the time, people were aware that cholera was a highly contagious disease but believed that the contagions traveled by air.

John Snow was an epidemiologist – a doctor who looks for patterns of information in order to identify causes. Snow's goal was to find a root cause for the disease in the afflicted neighbourhood. He worked tirelessly to gather the data that he could interpret as facts.

He discovered that the contagion by air theory fell apart because not everyone in the neighbourhood fell sick. He looked for things other than air that everyone who fell sick had in common. He found that all the homes where someone had become ill used a common water supply from the community well. John Snow's data led him to deduce that it was the contaminated well water that was making people sick.

John Snow's work was done in very limited and defined areas. He knew the data and facts to be true because it was collected by personal observations and conversations.

Today's situation is much different. Facebook has a billion members, all of whom have put up both personal statistics and also personal views on many matters. This data can be mined and analysed with modern algorithms and used for many purposes: some positive, like ecological and medical cures, but others negative, like cyberbullying, harmful hacking and identity theft. Today it is much harder to see the true sources of data that is shaping so many decisions around us.

Your initial analysis (select all that apply)

☐ John Snow took a huge risk in defying the conventional medical reasoning

☐ The source of the data used defines the outcome

☐ Much of the data used today is fake

☐ John Snow demonstrated that proper data is a major disruptor

☐ Good data is the engine of modern knowledge growth

Skillpod Insight

Many experts in the field suggest that data is the new energy driving the digital age. The reason for this is that it is now easy to build huge banks of data, and those banks can be fairly easily programmed to give back valuable information. Whoever owns that data and those analytic systems has a significant advantage over others. This is a major source of wealth for many corporations. Some of this data comes from monitoring businesses but much comes from personal online accounts. While there are benefits, like when your grocery store knows that you usually buy cat food on Mondays and sends you a coupon on Monday morning, it can also be very harmful when your information falls in the wrong hands, as we have seen with the Facebook scandal of 2018.

TIPS | Ask yourself these questions to get better at understanding the usefulness of data:

- ▸ Am I aware that data about me is being used without my permission?
- ▸ Do I think about what data I need to collect to make the best decisions?
- ▸ Do I have a good system for making the data I collect useful?
- ▸ Is it worth my while to review all the sites my information is on to assure it will not be used to harm me now or in the future?
- ▸ Do I have a way to gather relevant information from the internet, analyse it and use it productively?

Reflection:

Take a minute to reflect on a situation where you willingly gave up your data as a trade off of some kind. What was the situation? What was the benefit? Was it worth it? Write a few lines here.

DONE go back to your profile page and fill in a Information Management block or
NOT YET continue to the next scenario or jump to the Toolbox at the end of the chapter for more practice.

SCENARIO 4
Valuing digital privacy

Cesar considered himself pretty savvy about managing technology at work. The truth was that most of the routine work around security was done for him by IT. Files were regularly updated and old files deleted, firewalls were in place, passwords were secure and had to be changed regularly, o d apps were deleted from the system and remote access to the company server had a two-factor authentication. Cesar was scrupulous about conforming to the security requirements of a job he really valued.

The problem was that there was no transfer of learning from Cesar's professional use of technology to his personal use. His phone was not password protected and his favourite password for his online banking and shopping was Mephisto – the name of his dog, featured prominently on the dog's own Instagram account. And Cesar loved to be out there, the more outrageously the better. He was known for his over-the-top posts and tweets. He seemed to live his life, for better or worse, on social media.

You can probably write the final paragraph here yourself. Cesar ran into some very unfortunate problems which had a negative impact on his finances, reputation and job prospects. He couldn't figure out how a person as savvy as he considered himself to be about technology, could have been so badly damaged by data breaches and online rants.

Your initial analysis (select all that apply)

☐ Better privacy settings on his social media accounts would have prevented his problems

☐ Cesar should have been using the same privacy protections personally that he used at work

☐ Protecting his phone with a password would have solved all his problems

☐ Cesar should not have assumed he could post outrageous comments that would remain private

☐ Cesar didn't realize that everyone, consciously or not, is creating a digital footprint

Skillpod Insight

Cesar's situation, exaggerated as it seems to be here, is really not exceptional. Technology loves the naive or immature part of us – that part that convinces us that our passwords are good enough, that assures us that privacy settings in one place offer protection in other places, that makes us feel bad things will never happen to us, or that gives us the illusion of anonymity and privacy that allows us to behave badly toward others. Cesar was one person at work – careful, compliant, correct – and someone else entirely in his personal life. Guess which persona was known to most people, including his family and his employers?

Personal data is an asset. It can be sold to others without your permission, sometimes legally, but that is not always the case. There are different laws about privacy in different countries. And, of course, there is a whole hacking industry entirely outside the law. It grows in sophistication every day, as does our online usage in public places. Here is one rule of thumb: would you be comfortable with your parents or grandparents seeing everything that you post about yourself online? Know what you are putting up online, and always consider the consequences of things going wrong.

TIPS | Ask yourself these questions to get better at valuing digital privacy:

- ▶ Am I familiar with my privacy settings on my browser, social media sites and any public wifi systems that I use?
- ▶ Do I always select two-factor authentication when it is offered?
- ▶ Are all my devices password protected?
- ▶ Have I investigated using a Virtual Private Network (VPN) if I work on public WiFi?
- ▶ What is my strategy for building a positive digital footprint?
- ▶ Am I totally comfortable with the information/images about myself or others that I am putting online.

Reflection:

Take a minute to reflect on a situation in which a friend's privacy was violated because security or privacy settings were not in place. Write a few lines here.

DONE go back to your profile page and fill in a Information Management block or
NOT YET continue to the next scenario or jump to the Toolbox at the end of the chapter for more practice.

Congratulations!

You have completed the Information Management skill.

Self-Assessment:

Complete the following questions to assess your understanding of the material.

	COMPETENCY	YES	NOT YET
1	I always consider the sources when searching for and retrieving information.		
1	I am skillec at deciding what information is or is not important for a task.		
2	I manage social media, email and files without frustration.		
2	I have established good systems for storing and easily retrieving the information I need.		
3	I know how to find, use or collect data that will help me reach my goals.		
3	I am aware of how, when and why my personal data is collected.		
4	I take the appropriate steps to protect my personal information or intellectual property.		
4	I only share information that is not harmful to myself or to others.		

If you have answered **YES** to these questions, move on to the Information Management portfolio entry page. If you have answered **NOT YET**, reflect on where you are running into roadblocks in your understanding of the related competency and what you can do to address this. Create a simple plan to help you complete this skill.

The Toolbox

Use the following activities to dig deeper and continue to build your Information Management skills.

Judging sources: (est. 15 min.)

There is an expression, "garbage in, garbage out" from the early days of data management. It applies to all of us even now. If the source of information you are using is not appropriate to the task, then the information may be at best neutral, and at worst, harmful. Try to match the quality of the source to the task. Practise this by setting yourself an imaginary task, eg. you are about to purchase a car and for ethical reasons are committed to electric cars. You have a friend who drives an electric car and lives in Europe. Would she be a good source? Why or why not? What sources would you consult for each of the following categories of information you need?

- · Logistics - location of dealerships, charging
- · Performance - warranties, mileage/kilometerage, parts
- · Aesthetics and accessories

Establishing a good storage system: (est. 15 min.)

If you have successfully established a good storage system for files, it means that someone else with a minimum of instruction and some basic information about the nature and date of the files in question could find the correct version of any document, either in a filing system or on a screen. The tests for this are simple. Pretend you are writing a note to a colleague who will be taking over a file for you that you have given permission for them to retrieve. Whether in your real or virtual filing system you have 25 words to direct them to the correct version of the file once they have opened your cabinet or computer. How do you tell them where to find the file?

Considering sources of data: (est. 30 min.)

There are many sources of data, both primary and secondary. Different costs, effectiveness and reliability factors are associated with each kind. Test yourself by making a quick list of the most common forms of primary data and the most common forms of secondary data. If you can't do this yet, then look up the differences between them so that you are clear. Now, pretend you are opening a store in a rural town. You are trying to decide between opening a natural foods/health store or a convenience store. How might you use both primary and secondary data to ensure you make a good choice?

Restricting harmful data: (est. 1 hour)

The most common understanding of this comes from the news and social media sources of fake news and false facts. While these may not seem to affect you personally, you need to know how these things appear, how to avoid using them yourself and how to prevent them from hurting you. This exercise is to go on the web and find three main sources of fake news and three sources of deliberate lies that have intentionally hurt someone. Being aware is being prepared. What are three ways that you can protect yourself from harmful data?

Information Management Portfolio Entry

You are ready to create a portfolio piece that captures your own unique Information Management skill. Include skills-based language from the table below in your writing.

COMPETENCIES	ASSETS ("I...")
Choosing good sources	· consider my sources · select important information
Storing and retrieving of information	· manage my media and mail · have a good storage system
Understanding usefulness of data	· can identify relevant data points · am aware of sources of data
Valuing digital privacy	· protect my personal info · restrict data harmful to myself or others

STEP 1:

DEFINE
In your own words, define Information Management.

STEP 1 (Continued):

DEMONSTRATE:
Using skills-based language, describe one specific experience that captures your skill in this area.

You can also give an example of a skill or competency that you are working to develop.

ARTICULATE:
Why would an employer value your unique Information Management skills?

STEP 2:

CREATE
Use the portfolio guidelines in the appendix to create a Information Management portfolio entry.

STEP 3:

SHARE!
Feature this skill on your social media feed, your website, LinkedIn or online portfolio.

SKILL 6:
STRATEGIC THINKING

Strategic Thinking is deciding which of the possible approaches to a problem will result in the best outcomes.

Introduction

Just as you need the right tool for a carpentry task, you need the right thinking framework to complete any intellectual challenge. There isn't just one way to think – there is a repertoire of different thinking strategies from which you can select, depending on the context and the outcome you seek. In an era of rapid workplace change and the gig economy, it is important to have your eyes wide open, to be able to process and sort vast amounts of information, and to analyze and make decisions quickly. Knowing when to shift modes of thinking – e.g., from creative to strategic thinking – is a tool whose mastery is very helpful.

This is important for your success because employers are looking for employees who can think through challenges, generate ideas, make good evaluations of evidence, and produce reliable recommendations. Developing your abilities in the following competencies will start you on that path.

Competencies:

1 Respecting context
When and how to use contextual information to improve your thinking.

2 Thinking critically
Using a set of steps in which facts are gathered, analyzed, and evaluated in order to make a decision.

3 Planning and communicating strategically
Using the most relevant and convincing information to achieve a desired outcome.

4 Thinking locally and globally
Seeing the applicability of a good idea from one context to a totally new set of conditions or circumstances.

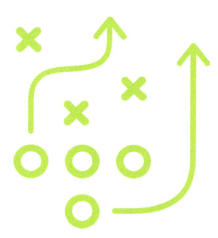

What employers value about strong Strategic Thinking skills:

► Sound judgment

► Process-oriented thinking and research

► Pattern finding, application of knowledge in new contexts

► Strategic communication

► Cultural and civic literacy

► Understanding of criteria

What entrepreneurs value about strong Strategic Thinking skills:

► 'Big picture' outlook

► Understanding context

► Ability to make difficult decisions

► Strategic communication

► Local to global frameworks

SCENARIO 1
Respecting context

Money has been set aside for a fitness facility in the new community centre. It is Juri's first challenge, working for the city, to develop the concept and budget and to present them in a neighbourhood association meeting. She researches diligently and develops a concept based on the space available, costs, and equipment ratings, and includes safety, durability, and ease of use. She gets a friend who is good with graphics to help her design a presentation deck that shows what the space will look like, the timeline, hours of operation, and support for classes and equipment use. She thinks she has a winner.

Juri decides to do a practice run with some of her team and the head of her division. It goes really well on her end but she notices their reaction is muted. Finally, her division head says, "Juri, you have done a lot of research and have put together an informative presentation. But you couldn't have consulted any of our community members because if you had, you would realize that many of the priorities of our diverse community are not reflected here. Some of our community, for religious and cultural reasons, will not respond well to open and mixed classes. We have a large population of seniors who will be intimidated by much of the equipment you have chosen and will be reluctant to use it. We know this from our history – six years ago, a similar layout failed in a local club for the same reason. Before we take this idea to our community, we need to talk to them and hear from them what they need."

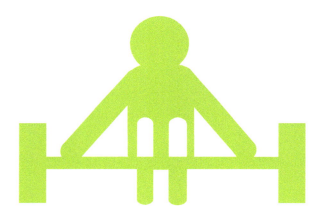

Your initial analysis (select all that apply)

- ☐ Juri got the response she hoped for
- ☐ Juri showed her presentation to the wrong group
- ☐ Juri's research was incomplete
- ☐ The community was not ready for the fitness facility
- ☐ Juri's design lacked empathy for the users

Skillpod Insight

Juri forgot to consider the context – to explore who was in the neighbourhood, their needs and desires, what previous attempts had been made to boost the community's health, and what other initiatives had been successful. Considerations such as history, geography, socio-economic and political realities, age, ethnicity, gender, and abilities are some of the issues of context that must have a bearing on the decisions we make and the initiatives we launch.

TIPS | Ask yourself these questions to get better at accommodating issues of context:

- ► Have I considered the needs, realities, and priorities of my audience/users?

- ► Have I run my ideas by those who are representative of my audience/users?

- ► Have I looked at and compensated for my own biases and experiences?

- ► Have I considered cause and effect?

- ► Is there a bigger picture, or broader set of circumstances, that should affect my recommendations?

Reflection:

Take a minute to reflect on a situation in which you effectively used or showed an understanding of context or wish that you had. Write a few lines here.

DONE go back to your profile page and fill in a Strategic Thinking block or
NOT YET continue to the next scenario or jump to the Toolbox at the end of the chapter for more practice.

Thinking critically

Clara is part of an interdepartmental team in a competitive and innovative firm. The company has recently invested heavily in research and development, with the result that department budgets are very tight. The team has a number of projects underway, each with a strongly vocal champion. All at the table have equal voices and it is their job to decide which projects have funding priority.

The first meeting is a nightmare. The team members who speak begin by pointing out the merits of the project they support. Some unintentionally belittle the work of other projects, even though they have been keen supporters of them in the past.

Seeing relationships being damaged, Clara knows that the team needs some structure in order to make the best decision, and that that structure needs to lead everyone in the same direction. Clara introduces a critical-thinking approach that will help them solve the budgeting problem. The team moves through each stage together, identifying the problem they have to solve, gathering market research and budget figures, then analyzing the data while considering the perspectives of other people with a stake in the outcome and the company's brand and mission. Going through this, they discover that one project stands out clearly from the rest. Working on that project first would actually give a boost to two of the other projects. The team unanimously agrees to a direction and implements a solution.

Your initial analysis (select all that apply)

☐ Clara worries too much about people's feelings

☐ The budget crisis should have been solved by cutting all projects equally

☐ A good process can produce better results and help the team's well-being

☐ Clara manipulated the group by using a process she knew would result in the outcome she wanted

☐ Clara's process was too restrictive – the team had no chance to be creative

Skillpod Insight

There are a number of other approaches Clara could have selected, but she knew her team was focused on the problem of prioritizing. She faced a problem-solving challenge with a group of people who were already threatened by the possible results of the discussion – this was not the climate for a lively creative-problem-solving exercise. Clara, rightly, focused on getting the team to assemble and analyze objective information and to determine a course of action from there by gradually eliminating options. Her goal was equally to strengthen the team's effectiveness and commitment and to get the best solution to the budget crunch.

Definition of critical thinking:

Critical thinking is the most commonly used thinking approach for academic tasks and relies chiefly on convergent thinking. It is highly structured, in five stages: identifying a problem, gathering and assessing evidence, considering other points of view, determining a course of action, and evaluating the outcome.

A model of the critical thinking approach:

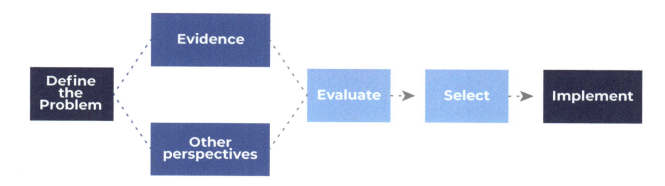

TIPS | Ask yourself these questions to get better at critical thinking:

- ▸ Can I define the problem I am trying to solve? Are there multiple ways of looking at it?
- ▸ What is the best evidence/data I can collect that relates to the problem?
- ▸ What other points of view exist that I should consider?
- ▸ With the above considerations in mind, what are the best ways to resolve this problem? What are the risks of each choice? What outcomes should I anticipate?
- ▸ How will I know I have succeeded in solving the problem? How will I evaluate success?

Reflection:

Take a minute to reflect on a situation in which you effectively used critical thinking. Write a few lines here.

DONE go back to your profile page and fill in a Strategic Thinking block or
NOT YET continue to the next scenario or jump to the Toolbox at the end of the chapter for more practice.

Planning and communicating strategically

Giles has developed an app that helps families who are interested in genealogy to pool their photos, official documents, letters, and stories. Trained as a librarian and very detail-oriented by nature, he knows the importance of being able to store and retrieve information with attention to both ease and security. He is confident that his app will find a market.

Through the business accelerator at a local community college, he gets the chance to present to a group of potential investors. He receives a package of information to help him plan. He will have twenty minutes to present and answer questions. The package contains thumbnail biographies of his panel of five investors and he learns three of them made their money in their own businesses and the other two inherited their wealth. Giles lays out a fifteen-minute presentation that begins with a short lesson in genealogical research and details some remarkable stories of families who have become deeply invested in learning about their own histories. It carefully takes the investors step by step through the navigation that permits secure storage and sharing of the records. During the presentation, Giles feels the attention of the listeners is wandering. The five remaining minutes are filled with one or two questions about how he got interested in this area. He finds out the next day that he has not been successful in attracting investor dollars.

Your initial analysis (select all that apply)

☐ The investors did not see the point of an app for genealogy

☐ We cannot tell from this description what Giles's strategy was

☐ Giles's communication plan did not take his listeners into account

☐ Giles did not allow enough time for questions

☐ Some of the investors' needs were not met in Giles's presentation

Skillpod Insight

This is a classic example of failing to match the communication plan and delivery to a strategy for success. Giles's job was not so much to educate his listeners about his field and his app as it was to persuade them that the idea was a robust one that would result in good returns on their investment. Whether those returns were in capital or social benefits really didn't matter. Giles focused his presentation on background, stories, and details of the app. Giles should have planned his presentation so that the key details – the existing demand, the field of competitors, the business case – were supported by the examples of background, family stories, and the details of the app that made it superior to anything else available. One of his family examples should have included one of the listeners in the room. This is really similar to thinking through the context piece, which was looked at earlier, with the added layer of applying strategy when you plan and communicate.

TIPS | Ask yourself these questions to get better at planning and communicating strategically:

- In 12 words or fewer, what is my strategic goal?
- What are the interests of my audience?
- What do I want their interests to be?
- What can I do to get my listeners on side in the first two minutes?
- Does my plan support my strategic goal?

Reflection:

Take a minute to reflect on a situation in which a strategy for communicating with a particular group made or would have made all the difference. Write a few lines here.

DONE go back to your profile page and fill in a Strategic Thinking block or
NOT YET continue to the next scenario or jump to the Toolbox at the end of the chapter for more practice.

SCENARIO 4
Thinking locally and globally

Fareed is a teacher of world studies and world politics in a large city, at a school close to the university. The university sponsors a Great Ideas challenge each year in which it poses a challenge faced by those in poverty, and invites teams to research the challenge and offer solutions. The winning team gets to work with members of the university community and NGOs to take their solution to the next step. Fareed has entered a student team in each of the past five years, with honourable mentions in the last two rounds.

This year's challenge is the issue of access to primary medical care for those in remote villages. Fareed's team is assigned an area in Uttar Pradesh in India, a densely populated state. The team is overwhelmed by the challenge – such huge numbers of people, such a lot of poverty, such traffic congestion on road and rail, and such distances between areas that provide medical services. They don't know where to start.

Sasha, one of the students, has just finished a business project on social entrepreneurship and shares with her team an idea she found in her research. A street charity in the US had refitted old buses with showers and basic medical care and was taking the services

to those living on the streets who did not want to go to the shelters. The project was very successful. Could this idea work in Uttar Pradesh?

The team members are divided about whether the two issues have enough in common, but finally agree on two patterns they see in common: on-site delivery and mobility. These two ideas provide focus for their research. They divide themselves into four groups: Partnerships, Village Culture, Health Needs, and Service Delivery. Do they have a chance of a successful outcome?

Your initial analysis (select all that apply)

- ☐ The team will not succeed without someone from India on the team
- ☐ The team needs to find the money to make any idea work
- ☐ The team will redefine their terms as they learn more
- ☐ The groups the team has chosen seem reasonable for the problem
- ☐ The solution for the homeless in the US has nothing to do with the problem the team is trying to solve

Skillpod Insight

The team has actually done a good job at anticipating many of the key approaches to using local/global thinking. They have found a pattern of similarity that will help to focus their research. They will doubtless have to change how they define mobility and what on-site delivery of service will entail. They have been shrewd about choosing their groups – failure to understand cultural differences contributes greatly to the failure of projects because projects cannot survive or scale without such considerations. The partnerships will promote understanding of what kind of primary medical care is needed and expertise in logistics will help with scaling the project and presenting a practical solution. This team has a good chance of coming up with a feasible, scalable solution.

TIPS | Ask yourself these questions to get better at local/global thinking on your projects:

- ▶ What cultural difference could prevent using an idea in a bigger or smaller context?
- ▶ What patterns do I see in a global issue that are similar to a local issue?
- ▶ What do I have to find out to design a good solution to a problem?
- ▶ What impact will scaling up or scaling down an idea have?
- ▶ What examples of innovation using local/global thinking could help move a project to the next level?

Reflection:

Take a minute to reflect on a situation in which you or others used thinking locally and globally to bring an effective or new solution to a problem. Write a few lines here.

DONE go back to your profile page and fill in a Strategic Thinking block or
NOT YET continue to the next scenario or jump to the Toolbox at the end of the chapter for more practice.

Congratulations!

You have completed the Strategic Thinking skill.

Self-Assessment:

Complete the following questions to assess your understanding of the material.

COMPETENCY		YES	NOT YET
1	I know what context is and why it matters.		
1	I understand how to separate cause and effect.		
2	I know how and when to use critical thinking.		
2	I can frame good questions when considering a problem.		
3	I have a strategic communication goal.		
3	I know what counts as good evidence in support of an idea.		
4	I am good at finding patterns of information.		
4	I can consider the implications of a national or global issue and anticipate similar local applications.		

If you have answered **YES** to these questions, move on to the Strategic Thinking portfolio entry page. If you have answered **NOT YET,** reflect on where you are running into roadblocks in your understanding of the related competency and what you can do to address this. Take a look a the Toolbox on the next page and try some of the exercises to deepen your understanding or mastery of the skill.

The Toolbox

Use the following activities to continue to build your Strategic Thinking skills.

Using the best evidence: (est. 3 hours)

Do an evidence check every time you write or speak about something that matters to you professionally or personally. Make a list of the evidence you have to support a particular point of view that you are sharing. Bracket anything you know to be a belief or opinion, rather than a fact. For the unbracketed items, track down a trusted source that corroborates each one. If you find opposing views, make sure you acknowledge them. Only use the facts you can corroborate. Use the beliefs and opinions but identify them as such – don't pretend they are factual. Use these tips to write one hypothetical blog post on a somewhat controversial topic.

Asking good questions: (est. 30 min.)

The key to asking good questions is to listen actively and deeply to what someone is saying. Do not focus on the chance to speak your view. Practise active listening. Listen to someone's point of view carefully. Before reacting to it, say "this is what I heard you say" or "am I right understanding" and then summarize their points or concerns, making sure that you have heard them accurately and not through a filter of your own bias. Listen with an intention of understanding. At the end, say "is that accurate?" When you get confirmation, you know you have the information you need to form good questions or points you wish to make in response. Try it out in a couple of conversations and see if it changes anything for you.

Critical thinking – using creative thinking strategies: (est. 30 min.)

You are thinking through a problem and you are stuck. Follow these steps:

▶ Share it with someone who has less specific knowledge of the situation than you do and ask them what they see or what they would do.

▶ Change your physical surroundings.

▶ Change the perspective by asking, "How would my mother, (my boss, my best friend, etc.) approach this?"

Communicate strategically: (est. 15 min.)

The next time someone (like your boss) tries to persuade you to do something, map their strategy:

▶ Write down the outcome they want.

▶ Write down in order each individual point they make.

▶ See whether you can link each point to the outcome.

This exercise will help you develop your strategic communication skills (although it might make you a pain to your friends!)

Local to global thinking: investigating other points of view: (est. 3 hours over 3 weeks)

Develop your curiosity about how other cultures and communities deal with their problems. Once a week, for three weeks, make an effort to find a problem that has been solved in another field, another culture or in another workplace. Read about it. Try to figure out how people went about solving it. You may not ever be able to use the actual solution they found but understanding the method they used may help you to broaden your own repertoire of problem-solving skills.

Strategic Thinking Portfolio Entry

You are ready to create a portfolio piece that captures your unique Strategic Thinking skill. Include skills-based language from the table below in your writing.

COMPETENCIES	ASSETS ("I...")
Respecting context	· consider the "bigger picture" · understand cause and effect
Thinking critically	· know the elements of critical thinking · ask good questions
Planning and communicating strategically	· have a strategic communication goal · know what counts as good evidence in support of an idea
Thinking locally and globally	· find patterns of information · think about ideas at a local and global level

STEP 1:

DEFINE

In your own words, define Strategic Thinking.

STEP 1 (Continued):

DEMONSTRATE:
Using skills-based language, describe one experience that captures your skill in this area.

ARTICULATE:
Why would an employer value your unique Strategic Thinking skills?

STEP 2:

CREATE
Use the portfolio guidelines in the appendix to create a Strategic Thinking portfolio entry.

STEP 3:

SHARE!
Feature this skill on your social media feed, website, and LinkedIn and online profiles.

SKILL 7:
DESIGN & INNOVATION

Design is a creative problem solving process that can help lead to innovative outcomes.

Design Thinking is a five-part process that starts with empathy (understanding the end user), problem definition, ideation (creative brainstorming), prototyping a solution, and iteration (testing and revision).

Introduction

Societies, cultures, and civilizations are built upon innovation. The Romans were innovative engineers, the Greeks were innovative scientific and philosophical thinkers. The old economy was founded on mass production and repetitive labour functions. The new economy is being built on improving existing products, and creating new categories of products and ways to live in our world, at such accelerated cycles that innovation is a requirement. Understanding and applying the design process can help produce innovative products, services, and systems that position the end user at the centre of the problem-solving process. Design is the process for realizing the outcome. Innovation is the result of creative thinking.

Competencies:

1 **Learning from empathy**
You are able to understand a problem from another person's perspective. This is the key to human-centred design.

2 **Identifying problems**
You have considered a problem from several perspectives, separated the problem from the symptoms, identified biases, and come up with a robust problem definition.

3 **Thinking divergently and convergently**
Divergent thinking: you know several methods of creative thinking and when to use them.
Convergent thinking: you know how to sort and determine which ideas are most appropriate to the problem.

4 **Iterating**
Your prototyping cycle plans for several iterations based on end-user feedback rather than extensive research producing one final product with no feedback.

What employers value about strong Design & Innovation skills:

- ► Creative problem-solving
- ► Ability to identify the right problem for the right people
- ► Global thinking/systems thinking
- ► Ability to seek and work with feedback
- ► Ability to move from ideas to action
- ► Shorter product/services development cycles

What entrepreneurs value about strong Design & Innovation skills:

- ► Creative problem-solving
- ► Ability to identify the right problem for the right people
- ► Global thinking/systems thinking
- ► Ability to seek and work with feedback
- ► Ability to move from ideas to action
- ► Shorter product/services development cycles

SCENARIO 1
Learning from empathy

Global water, sanitation, and hygiene problems are massive. Just under one billion people do not have easy access to clean water. Nearly one third of the globe does not have access to toilets. The crisis has a debilitating impact on health, and social and economic situations of many people around the globe. Liu lives in Toronto and has become very interested in this issue. He took a job at a not-for-profit organization that was raising funds to build clean-water wells and latrines for a small community in South Asia. Liu organized a fundraising campaign that successfully raised the funding needed. Liu and his team decided how many latrines they could afford and what models seemed best suited to the location. They celebrated the success with the donors, shared the action plan, and, the following month, the team boarded a plane. Once in South Asia, they participated in the build. It took two months in very hot conditions but finally the borehole was dug and the public latrines were installed. Liu and his team returned home and reported on their success with an evening event showing video of the construction and happy faces.

Three years later, Liu had an opportunity to travel to South Asia again and, while there, traveled to the latrine project community to see how things had progressed. The village leaders took him to the latrines and to Liu's shock, the small structure was being used as a chicken coop. He turned to the village leaders, jaw on the ground, and wondered what had happened and how he would report back to his donors.

Your initial analysis (select all that apply)

- ☐ Liu mismanaged the project
- ☐ The community really needed a chicken coop and not latrines
- ☐ Liu was deliberately misled by the village leaders
- ☐ The latrines were in the wrong place
- ☐ The latrines were not designed with empathy for the users

Skillpod Insight

This is a story that is sadly far too common in the world of development aid. Well-meaning people raise funding for projects and decide how this money should be spent, without understanding the context or needs of the end user. Unfortunately, the model of latrine that was chosen was too dangerous and challenging to use for children, the elderly, and those with physical challenges. The chosen location was too far from town. The route was dark and left everyone vulnerable to snakes and other predators. If the team had gone to the site beforehand, they could have talked to a wide range of end users, including the most vulnerable. They could have tried walking the route in the day and night, in good weather and bad, to understand the problem from the perspective of the most vulnerable people. At the very least, they could have selected representatives from various groups and asked them to talk about their experiences and challenges, and extracted insights to help create a plan for a more inclusive and effective solution.

TIPS | Ask yourself these questions to get better at starting with empathy when developing services and products:

▸ What do I know about the end users? Have I talked and really listened to them?

▸ Have I allowed the end users to tell me a story about their experiences (rather than a directed interview)?

▸ Have I designed an experience to put myself in the shoes of the end users? (For example, simulate a sight impairment with a blindfold.)

▸ Have I designed an observation session in which I can watch users in action to see how they currently manage the challenge presented?

Reflection:

Take a minute to reflect on a situation in which you used empathy to understand the problem from the perspective of the end user when trying to creatively solve a problem. Write a few lines here.

DONE go back to your profile page and fill in a Design & Innovation block or
NOT YET continue to the next scenario or jump to the Toolbox at the end of the chapter for more practice.

SCENARIO 2
Problem identification

Randi and Theo are graphic designers. They have been hired by The Cake Museum to design their website. The Cake Museum is a small niche museum, displaying cakes from all different cultures and events. It was originally located in the home of Ms. Penny. Ms. Penny was a lifelong baker who became a legend for her creations. In 2015, her collection was turned into a not-for-profit cultural organization and moved into a permanent home in a suburban location. The new location makes the Cake Museum a destination but also limits the number of visitors who are able to come.

The designers were struck by the potential to have fun with this project. They knew that they could deliver the website on time and on budget. They talked to the client about their needs for the website, proposed concepts, and completed the job. At the final meeting, the client said that they liked the website and it worked fine but it was not particularly innovative and didn't do anything very "interesting." The designers walked away upset and confused.

Your initial analysis (select all that apply)

☐ There was more to the client's problem than they had said

☐ The website was actually not well executed

☐ Randi and Theo were not good designers

☐ The client had unrealistic expectations

☐ Randi and Theo could not be expected to be mind-readers

Skillpod Insight

In the meeting with the client, there is no mention of Randi and Theo digging deeper into the client's request. They forgot to ask the most important questions – why? Why did the client want a website? What were they hoping to achieve? Why does this problem exist? Clients can't always articulate their problem clearly and it is your job to ask these important questions. In this case, Randi and Theo got carried away with novelty and forgot to push themselves to discover the true problem that was giving rise to the client's frustration.

TIPS | Challenge yourself to respond to these questions to get better at problem identification:

- ▶ What is the most obvious problem? Are there secondary or tertiary problems?
- ▶ How do I know this is a problem?
- ▶ Can I separate cause and effect?
- ▶ Have I identified my own bias and assumptions relating to this problem? Would others look at it differently?
- ▶ Have I identified for whom this is a problem and created a character sketch/persona of the end user?

Reflection:

Take a minute to reflect on a situation in which you did not correctly identify a problem. What were the consequences? What methods could you have used to help get to the root problem? Write a few lines here.

DONE go back to your profile page and fill in a Design & Innovation block or
NOT YET continue to the next scenario or jump to the Toolbox at the end of the chapter for more practice.

SCENARIO 3
Divergent and convergent thinking

At a large bank head office, there is an opportunity in the product-innovation team to develop a game that will help encourage collaboration. This will be presented to the president at the internal AGM. This new project is announced at the Monday morning meeting and anyone who is interested can join the initial brainstorm session that will take place at a working lunch. There are three women who are great friends. Everyone knows that they will show up. These women went to high school together and are connected through a tight network. It was a coincidence that they all wound up in the same working group at the bank but their friendship makes the group lively and they can always be counted on to participate.

The first lunch meeting goes well. The three friends are the only participants and a lively brainstorming session takes pace. Lots of Post-it Notes are used to document the ideas and all three leave feeling energized. At the next lunch meeting, three new people join. The three friends take charge and present their previous ideas. The group decides to do more brainstorming to include the new people. Some in the new group are shy

but eventually they present their ideas too. Tensions arise when the shy group feels like their ideas are being dismissed. At the third meeting, they decide to mix the groups and do another brainstorming round to gather more ideas. By the fourth lunch session, the group is overwhelmed with ideas and the tension explodes. One from the shy group starts shouting that no one is listening and nothing is getting done. What went wrong?

Your initial analysis (select all that apply)

☐ This was not the right group or mix of personalities for the task

☐ The three friends should have been left alone to develop an idea for the game

☐ The three friends need to find a way to be more open to the ideas of others. There does not seem to be any structure to the process

☐ The whole group was likely frustrated by the lack of progress

---

Skillpod Insight

You don't often have control over who gets to participate in group projects in the workplace. This is especially challenging when you are tasked with producing an innovative idea, product, or service. While some people are naturally more out-of-the-box thinkers, and natural collaborators, there are elements of the innovation process that can be learned. This group would have benefited from having a defined process that allocated time for creative thinking (divergent), a process for sorting and selecting ideas (convergent,) and an approach for managing "creative abrasion." Creative abrasion is the tension that can arise when people with different expertise, skill sets, or opinions actively challenge, debate, and argue in a framework that has the goal of producing a novel outcome. This can be a very difficult process and requires a foundation of respect from all participants. In the innovation process, creative abrasion must be embraced as it is often the source of true innovation, but it can be painful if not managed well. In our bank scenario, this group was not properly prepared and is unlikely to be able to be successful.

TIPS | Ask yourself these questions to get better at knowing where and when to use divergent and convergent thinking:

▶ It is important to clarify a goal. Is the goal to come up with a broad range of new ideas or to sort and evaluate ideas that are already on the table?

▶ Remind yourself or the group that the first twenty ideas will provide the most common solutions. Innovative solutions take work and the input of diverse viewpoints.

▶ Have I used research at appropriate times to push my ideas further?

▶ Do I have some objective criteria to help evaluate the ideas?

▶ Do I have some tools to manage and embrace creative abrasion?

Reflection:

Take a minute to reflect on a situation where you may have used divergent (brainstorming) and convergent (selection criteria) thinking to come up with a creative solution. Write a few lines here.

DONE go back to your profile page and fill in a Design & Innovation block or
NOT YET continue to the next scenario or jump to the Toolbox at the end of the chapter for more practice.

SCENARIO 4
Iteration

Ravi has been hired to manage the development of a new app for his employer, a medical product company. The app is intended to share important stories/news/research about the company's expertise and successes. It is not a technically complicated app and will be a marketing tool primarily targeting an external audience. Ravi has one junior graphic designer, Lynn, working with him. Ravi develops a workback plan, establishing deadlines and a final launch date – six months down the road. Ravi gets approval for the work plan from his supervisor. The team of two are excited by the prospect of taking on this new project.

Ravi creates a strategic plan that outlines which stories they want to capture, who they need to interview, and which assets they need to collect. Lynn is researching parallel examples to analyze how they can differentiate themselves from the competition while learning from industry best practices. They throw themselves completely into developing this new product with energy and zeal. They meet their milestones and are on track to launch the app on time and on budget. They have completed one test on the final version of

the app with their intimate group, who gave very positive reviews, and are working on minor, final revisions. One week before the launch date, the supervisor tells them that an app no longer seems like the right solution. In addition, the stories they have created feature products that the company is no longer producing. The project is done and looks fantastic but it does not launch. Ravi and Lynn are stunned, realizing that their work over six months – all the writing, design, photography, video, great collaborative process they developed, and the interviews – has been useless. What went wrong?

Your initial analysis (select all that apply)

☐ This was really bad luck

☐ The team should have done more research

☐ This project was poorly managed

☐ Ravi and Lynn were overly committed to one solution

☐ There should have been some way of moving faster through the development cycle

Skillpod Insight

This really is rotten luck, but it also reflects the reality of the current rapid pace of change and the flaws in a traditional product-development cycle. Ravi (and his supervisor) should have employed a rapid prototyping approach, which could have produced a workable prototype or demonstration of the product within two weeks. In the iterative process, the team designs a prototype and outlines clear goals for its testing. Are they looking to validate their idea? Get feedback on the nature of the content? The user experience? All of these are important. The worst thing to do is to wait until the prototype is completed and then show it to friends who may be reluctant to give anything but encouraging feedback such as "I really like it." This kind of feedback is useless to the development process as it is not constructive and may not even be honest. In addition, in this case, there was too much time spent researching early in the process and feedback came too late in the cycle. With the iterative process there is a plan, but the team also needs to make room for uncertainty and change. They need to focus on getting working prototypes into the hands of the end users as early as possible to capture feedback and incorporate it into the next iteration. Research is folded into the process as prototypes are made and feedback is given. In the current economy there really is no such thing as a finished product. As they say, the only constant is change.

TIPS | Ask yourself these questions to get better at applying an iterative prototyping process:

- ► How can I prototype and test my idea with the end user within the next two weeks?
- ► What are my prototype testing goals?
- ► Practically, how will I capture feedback? Video? Interviews?
- ► How do I make sure that the feedback is honest and constructive?
- ► Have I limited initial background research and instead allowed for research time to be distributed throughout the product/service development process?

Reflection:

Take a minute to reflect on a situation where you may have used an iterative process or could have benefited from this approach. Write a few lines here.

DONE go back to your profile page and fill in a Design & Innovation block or
NOT YET continue to the next scenario or jump to the Toolbox at the end of the chapter for more practice.

Congratulations!

You have completed the Design & Innovation skill.

Self-Assessment:

Complete the following questions to assess your understanding of the material.

COMPETENCY		YES	NOT YET
1	When identifying a problem, I listen to and observe those closest to the problem.		
1	I can create an experience that puts me in the shoes of those closest to the problem.		
2	When someone asks me to solve a problem, I ask lots of questions to try to understand all dimensions of the issue.		
2	I can identify my bias and assumptions.		
3	I know how and when to be creative in my thinking.		
3	I use criteria to help me decide which idea to pursue.		
4	When developing a new idea, product, or service, I think about how to make a test of this as quickly as possible.		
4	I seek feedback on ideas as early as possible.		

If you have answered **YES** to these questions, move on to the Design & Innovation portfolio entry page. If you have answered **NOT YET,** reflect on where you are running into roadblocks in your understanding of the related competency and what you can do to address this. Take a look a the Toolbox on the next page and try some of the exercises to deepen your understanding or mastery of the skill.

The Toolbox

Use the following activities to continue to build your Design & Innovation skills.

Empathy: (est. 30 min.)

Empathy is understanding what matters to others by putting yourself in their shoes. For a long time, designers created mass goods because everyone wanted all the conveniences. Now, the move is toward personalized products. Artificial intelligence and 3D printing drive this trend. This exercise is focused on what is involved in personalized service that meets the needs of consumers or beneficiaries of services. The exercise is to find one example of design that is somehow focused on a user experience (good or bad). This can be architecture, web, or app design, product or fashion. Assess how much empathy was taken into consideration in the design.

Problem identification: (est. 30 min.)

Note: this is best done with more than one person.

We all know instances of serious problems left unsolved because those in charge did not identify the real problem. Often it is much easier to identify the symptoms. One great exercise to help find the root cause is to use the Five Whys questioning technique developed by Sakichi Toyoda in the 1930s. When thinking about a problem, ask yourself (or have someone ask you) "why?" The first response will be the most obvious but not the root cause. Keep asking and responding to the question why five times and ultimately you should get closer to the true root cause.

Divergent/convergent thinking: (est. 1 hour)

Note: best done with more than one person.

When a person or organization proposes plans for a new service or facility, they usually have visualized the outcome they want. Often what the leader is looking for is consensus for their vision of the outcome. Unless you are Steve Jobs, this is not a guaranteed path to innovative ideas. Divergent thinking is a creative process of throwing open the doors and creating myriad ideas without any judgement. It is creative brainstorming. Convergent thinking is the process of sorting through and filtering all those ideas to arrive at the best solution. The next time you need to brainstorm, use the 100-ideas technique. Give yourself a time limit of fifteen minutes and challenge yourself to come up with 100 solutions no matter how crazy, impractical, or plain ridiculous. Once you have your 100 ideas, establish some criteria for narrowing down the selection – e.g., which are the most original, fun, interactive. You decide and come up with three criteria to help select the best solutions.

Iteration: (est. 30 min.)

Very few plans, projects, or models work out the way they are first planned. A single iteration is just one idea for success and often not a lasting or innovative solution. Multiple iterations flush out the flaws. Legend has it that James Dyson and his team worked for five years and made over 5,000 prototypes before hitting success with his revolutionary vacuum. One big flaw is not recognizing the perspectives of others (empathy). Another is using the wrong materials or addressing a problem you have but others don't. This exercise is to find one example of a plan, project, or product that hits upon success thanks to a process of iteration. Do you have personal plans that have used iteration to succeed or radically change? Write about them.

Design & Innovation Portfolio Entry

You are ready to create a portfolio piece that captures your unique Design & Innovation skill. Include skills-based language from the table below in your writing.

COMPETENCIES	ASSETS ("I...")
Learning from empathy	· know who I am designing for · can create an empathetic experience
Identifying problems	· know how to get to the root cause · can identify bias anc assumption
Thinking convergently and divergently	· know how and when to be creative · have criteria to help with idea selection
Iterating	· test new ideas quickly · can seek and incorporate feedback

STEP 1:

DEFINE
In your own words, define Design & Innovation skills.

STEP 1 (Continued):

DEMONSTRATE:
Using skills-based language, describe one experience that captures your skill in this area.

ARTICULATE:
Why would an employer value your unique Design & Innovation skills?

What does it mean to be a
creative problem solver?

STEP 2:

CREATE
Use the portfolio guidelines in the appendix to create a Design & Innovation portfolio entry.

STEP 3:

SHARE!
Feature this skill on your social media feed and website, and your LinkedIn or online portfolio.

Summarizing Your Skills

Use this page to make notes to help write clear responses to the interview questions on the following page. Write point form, or rough versions here and use the next page for well written and clearly articulated full-sentence responses.

It is common to fall back on old beliefs and opinions when responding to these questions. Remember to put into practice all that you have learned so far when responding to these questions. This includes using skills-based language and points that you have learned from the scenarios. Draw on your reflections and portfolio entries when you describe your skills. Think about how you could support each statement with specific evidence.

How Well Do You Know Yourself and Your Skills Now?

Now that you have completed the skills program, responding to these questions should prove easier and more fruitful. Use your skill and competency language and personal asset key words to respond to these four main questions once again.

Compare the responses to the first time and recognize how far you have come.

Name:

1 **Tell me about yourself.**
What are the first three things that you would say if someone asked you about you?

1.

2.

3.

2 **What are your top three strengths?**

1.

2.

3.

3 **What weaknesses do you have, gaps are you working to fill, or skills are you continuing to build?**

1.

2.

4 **What is the number-one value you bring to this organization?**
Why should I consider hiring you?

1.

The PLP
Personal Learning Preferences

Learning is a skill, like writing, soccer, or painting, that we can improve with applied effort. However, everyone learns differently. Do you know how you learn best?

The Personal Learning Preferences (PLP) assessment can help you uncover your learning style. It can be used as a tool to help you leverage your strengths when you need to learn a new skill or complete a task. Knowing your PLP can help reduce frustration and increase success.

The PLP provides a customized overview of your preferences at this moment in time based on your responses to a series of questions. Your preferences will fall within four areas, which we call quadrants. Each quadrant relates to a specific set of strengths. The combined quadrants include all skills that are required to complete a project or task. Most people have strengths in multiple quadrants but it is rare to have equal strengths in all four quadrants.

This inventory of strengths is neither static nor permanent. It will evolve as you grow, learn, and respond to dynamics in your environment.

Go to www.skillpod.ca to complete the PLP assessment.

There are three types of information that are blended to produce your profile:

Role Preferences

You will be asked forced-choice questions to help define your preferred role.

Personal Interests

It is important to think about things that already interest you as these can influence your learning preferences or help you create a learning environment that will be engaging to you. The personal interests listed in the assessment suggest a preference for various quadrants.

Multiple Intelligences

In 1983, Dr. Howard Gardner of Harvard University argued that the traditional definition of intelligence needed to expand. He developed a system defining eight different intelligences that he felt more accurately captured human potential. These include: kinesthetic (physical intelligence), naturalist (natural environment), interpersonal (social intelligence), intrapersonal (self-knowledge), verbal (language intelligence), spatial (visual and pattern recognition), musical, and mathematical/logical. Drawing on the work of Stephen J. Gould and Robert Sternberg, we also include practical intelligence (the ability to get things done). These concepts were central in the creation of a seminal learning resource program in Canada created in collaboration with Drs. J m Anderson and Linda Siegel of the McMaster University Medical Centre, and a teacher, Jay Parry, in the mid-1980s. It has had lasting results and has expanded to many schools.

The Quadrants

Your PLP will be displayed on a chart showing strength in a particular quadrant. The quadrants are set out counter-clockwise, as in the mathematical quadrants.

Quadrant 1 (Q1)

Q1 relates to deep thinking and a facility with abstract ideas and abstract reasoning. Quadrant 1 learners tend to learn best through words and imagination. They think logically. They use abstract/verbal skills.

The Oxford dictionary defines "abstract" as existing in thought or as an idea but not having a physical or concrete existence, like love or beauty. People with a high score in Q1 are good at analyzing and researching and often dive deeply into the details of a project before addressing the big picture.

If you find your strengths here, you may be one of those who is very determined to find and get the facts right. You may find it easy to analyze information with abstract mathematical or scientific models. These are models you think about in your head, but they can be hard to learn or use. You may also often find yourself lost in thought. Poets can be found here, as they are thinking about abstract ideas, and are often in a world of their own creation, full of metaphors and imagery. You will find accountants, financial experts, math teachers and professors, puzzle solvers, computer programmers, and people who deal with minute details.

Professions typically with strong skills in Q1:
Administrators and organizers of big events, mathematicians, financial analysts, corporate lawyers, poets.

Famous people who display characteristics we would associate with Q1 learning:
It is not easy to find famous Q1 people because they tend to stay behind the scenes. Most are busy researching, analyzing data, and producing reports. Examples would include policy researchers for UNESCO or Statistics Canada, the NASA mathematician Katherine Johnson, made famous by the film "Hidden Figures," a country's minister of finance, or the Persian poet Rumi.

Quadrant 2 (Q2)

Q2 relates to spoken and visual language skills with a focus on purposeful, practical goals. Quadrant 2 learners tend to learn best through words and practical activities. They think about relationships. They use concrete/verbal skills.

People with a high score in Q2 have strong language skills and are good at presenting. They are good at communicating and marketing. They are happy to discuss learning with others and learn by teaching and sharing knowledge. Combining Q2 strengths with interpersonal intelligence can be powerful.

Professions typically with strong skills in Q2:
Social media experts, church pastors, politicians, journalists, YouTube personalities, actors, politicians, authors (e.g., of popular novels), salespeople, coaches, trainers, promoters, journalists, playwrights.

Famous people who display characteristics we would associate with Q2 learning:
Oprah (celebrity), Michelle Obama (former First Lady, author), Gary Vaynerchuk (media guru/entrepreneur), J. K. Rowling (Harry Potter author), Justin Trudeau (world leader), Mohandas Gandhi (world leader).

Quadrant 3 (Q3)

Q3 relates to graphic and physical skills with a focus on purposeful, practical goals. Quadrant 3 learners tend to learn best through visual images and hands-on activities. They think about practical tasks. They use concrete/graphic skills.

People with a high score in Q3 are strong at building models, creating images and graphs, and using pictures to explain or understand important topics. They prefer to work from images and graphic plans rather than from manuals or lectures. They may be more kinesthetically inclined. You will find here builders, craftspeople. engineers, tradespeople, athletes – in other words, all those who are active in getting things done. These learners may have some trouble in school as much of the high school teaching moves towards the verbal and abstract. Learners in this quadrant will prefer to get on with it. The danger is that the 'it' may not be clearly defined. Make sure the goal is clear!

Professions typically with strong skills in Q3:
Crafts people of all kinds (beer, wine, textiles, ceramics, etc.), engineers, athletes, cooks, dancers, explorers, security professionals, trades people.

Famous people who display characteristics we would associate with Q3 learning:
Jamie Oliver (chef), LeBron James (basketball player), Serena Williams (tennis player), Mike Holmes (construction/TV personality), Simone Giertz (YouTube Inventor), Anthony Bourdain (chef, explorer).

Quadrant 4 (Q4)

Q4 relates to graphic and abstract reasoning skills with a focus on seeing patterns and connecting the dots. Quadrant 4 learners are good at seeing the bigger picture. They tend to learn through visual images, diagrams and their imagination. They think about the bigger picture. They use graphic/abstract skills.

These people can easily use pictures to make their points. These pictures can be plans of spaces, buildings, theatre stage settings, etc. They can also combine the images and thoughts as in children's graphic story books or graphic novels. Architects, like Daniel Libeskind, design buildings not just as physical spaces, but also as intellectual and challenging ideas.

Professions typically with strong skills in Q4:
Set-designers, artists, designers, architects, physicists, graphic novelists, elite sports coaches, systems analyst.

Famous people who display characteristics we would associate with Q4 learning:
Theodor Geisel otherwise known as Dr. Seuss (children's author), stage director Julie Taymor (of The Lion King), Stephen Hawking (physicist), Ai Weiwei (artist), Annie Leibovitz (photographer), Zaha Hadid (architect), Paula Scher (graphic designer/illustrator), Art Spiegelman (graphic novelist).

*Note: The categorization of people's learning preferences listed above is based purely on observation and used to help explain the characteristics typical of, and the differences between the quadrants.

 Go to Skillpod.ca and complete your PLP.

How to use your PLP

Your PLP results will tell you where your learning preferences lie and provide an overview of your quadrant's characteristics. Read on to discover how to use this strength to your advantage when starting a new task or learning challenge.

1. Tackling a learning challenge

For example, you have decided (or your boss has decided) that you should learn something new, such as a language, software, a skill, etc. Your best chance of success is to start from your comfort zone. The next time you have a learning challenge, think about how you can design the learning to build on your strengths.

For example, a Q1 learner may choose to begin by reading an instruction manual. A Q2 learner may want to talk to someone they know who has expertise in the area. A Q3 learner might want to build a prototype or roll up her sleeves and give it a try, while a Q4 learner may want to create a diagram mapping out the big picture and context before diving into details of the task. If you get frustrated while trying to learn something new, you may not be using a strengths-based approach. Explore options for learning in different ways.

2. Starting a new project or task

Understanding your PLP can also help you overcome common challenges when starting a new task. In school, teachers will most often tell you that the right way to begin an assignment is by planning it. This is great if you have strengths in Q1. However, for those who have strengths in Q2, Q3, and Q4, this may be more frustrating than productive, as it is not starting in a comfort zone. It might be less frustrating to start from your strength, build momentum, and work back around to the more challenging areas. Or to find some help with planning (Q1) before using your strength if it lies in another area.

3. Project management

Almost all projects require the full range of quadrant-based skills, from planning to seeing patterns and adding context, to execution and sharing the information. If you do not have skills in all quadrants, you may need to build them. Consider whether you need to improve in any specific areas to be able to complete the task or learning that is in front of you. Alternatively, you can also try to fill this gap with help from someone who has strengths in these missing quadrant areas.

4. Teamwork

The PLP provides you with self-knowledge. It will also help you understand others around you and potentially help mitigate conflict by revealing that collaborators are not trying to be difficult; they really do think differently from you. Armed with the PLP, you can build teams with diverse skills and use strengths to help achieve team goals.

Learning is not just about taking more courses. Rather, it is about carefully observing and experimenting with how you find, analyze, and learn new information effectively in order to identify a system that works best for you. The best way to gain an understanding of how you learn is to look at things you do and try to understand what worked and what could be improved. Finally, understanding that people around you are learning in very different ways may help reduce unnecessary stress in group/teamwork.

The PLP is dynamic and will likely shift depending on various factors in your life. The important thing is to know where you are and to work to leverage the strengths of your PLP to learn faster and smarter.

APPENDIX 2
Creating a Portfolio Entry

The portfolio entry consists of both a visual component (e.g., an image) and words (e.g., written or spoken). With that as a foundation, feel free to get as creative as you like. The writing should be strategic and persuasive in tone (i.e., not journal writing) and have the goal of convincing an employer that you have the skill or competency presented.

It will be very difficult to create the portfolio entry without having first completed the skill chapter, especially the final skill reflection page

(Step 1: Define, Demonstrate, Articulate). Once you have completed the skill chapter and Step 1, it should not take more than fifteen minutes to write the entry.

When it comes to choosing an image, the most powerful images are ones that you have created or that show you in action. If you use an image that is not yours, remember to only use images that you have permission to use. Even images from sources like Creative Commons need to be credited.

Use one of the two examples below as a general guide to help create a portfolio entry.

Option 1:

Use these sentences as a guide to write a paragraph about your knowledge for one skill.

- ▶ Here is why [SKILL] is (pick one – tough, crucial, overlooked, important, etc.).
- ▶ Here is a time I experienced it (give one specific example)
- ▶ As a result of my focus on [SKILL or COMPETENCY], here are two things that happened.
- ▶ Had I not focused on [SKILL or COMPETENCY], here is what might have happened.
- ▶ A concluding comment about the value this brings to the work you do.

Example:

Information Management is crucial for me as a recent graduate looking for work. While I was talking to a prospective employer, she told me that she found a link to a number of YouTube videos that I had created when I was younger. This was not the professional image that I hoped to share. As a result, I have carefully searched and changed privacy settings on my social media to make sure that I have better managed my personal image. I know that care and attention to privacy is important for me and those around me and that it will reflect how I care about the company and my colleagues.

Option 2:

Pick one competency and one tip. Create a six-sentence script of no more than 100 words.

- ▶ Topic sentence: define the skill in your words.
- ▶ The claim: elaborate on the topic sentence – why it matters.
- ▶ The evidence: one example from your life or the world around you.
- ▶ Explain the evidence: e.g., consequences of doing this well or poorly.
- ▶ The other point of view or more evidence.
- ▶ The wrap-up: how this adds value to your work or would add value to an employer.

Example:

Empathy is a critical element of human-centred design when designing new products or services. Empathy requires that the end user is included in the design process. If I were designing something for an elderly person, I would spend time observing them. I would have them tell me a story that relates to the issue (e.g., mobility). I would ask questions and listen carefully. Finally, when I have a prototype ready, I would ask them to test it and give me feedback. This way, I will not base my work on assumptions but on really understanding the problem from the user's perspective. I bring an understanding of empathy to all the work that I do.

PORTFOLIO TIPS	EXAMPLES
Provide a credit for the source of the image used if this is not yours.	E.g., Photo by rawpixel.com from Pexels.
Put yourself in the shoes of an employer. What would they think if they read your portfolio entry?	E.g., "Wow, this candidate has great teamwork skills."
Use at least five words from the skill-competency-assets diagram.	E.g., For a portfolio entry about Teamwork, my entry included the words: roles and norms, integrity, manage conflict, team goals, outcomes.
Summarize how this skill would be a benefit to any work environment, demonstrating that this is a transferable skill.	E.g., "I know that care and attention to privacy are important for me and those around me, and also will reflect on how I care about the company and my colleagues."
Ask yourself if you are presenting an opinion or generalities or clear facts supported by evidence.	Generality or opinion-based example: I am careful about privacy on my social media because there are a lot of hackers out there. Evidence-based example: While I was talking to a prospective employer, she told me that she found a link to a number of YouTube videos that I had created when I was younger.

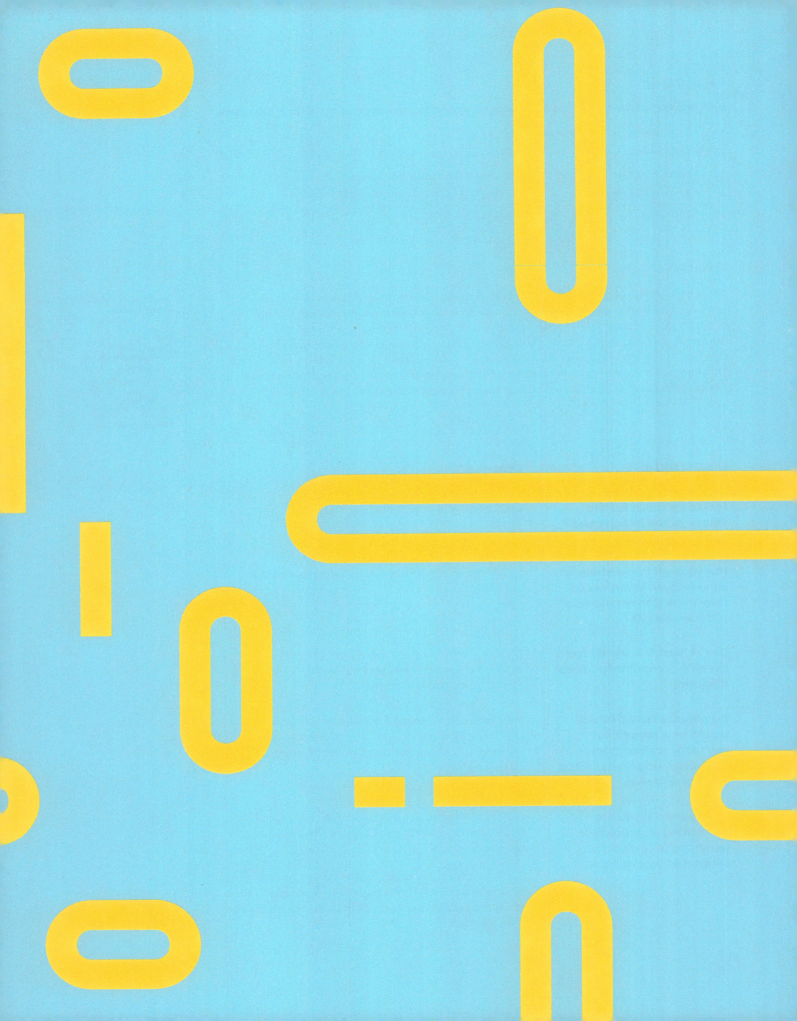

CPSIA information can be obtained
at www.ICGtesting.com
Printed in the USA
BVHW021921030720
582834BV00002B/11